AF588512

Krakow – New York – Virginia

GIRLS + EGGS

Contemporary Art Against Reproductive Injustice

By Siona Wilson
With additional essays by:
Alyson Bardsley, Jane Marcus-Delgado, and Beth Hinderliter

Participating Artists:
Michael Biber | Martyna Borowiecka | Danni O'Brien | Magda Buczek | Kat Chamberlin
Moyra Davey | Piotr Dłużniewski | Monika Drożyńska | Pippa Garner | Jakub Hošek
Maria Kniaginin-Ciszewska | Maja Krysiak | Bartek Arobal Kociemba | Oskar Korsár
Peter Kunt | Madeline Kuzak | Beatrix Reinhardt | Mira Schor | Agnieszka Szostek

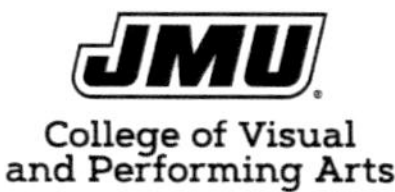

DUKE HALL
GALLERY OF
FINE ART

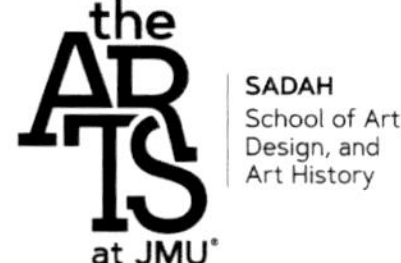

This catalog accompanies an exhibition that was on display at James Madison University from January 30th to March 8th, 2024.

Duke Hall Gallery of Fine Art
820 S. Main Street.
Harrisonburg, VA 22807
P: 540.568.6407
http://www.jmu.edu/dukehallgallery/

ISBN 978-163944273-7

Table of Contents

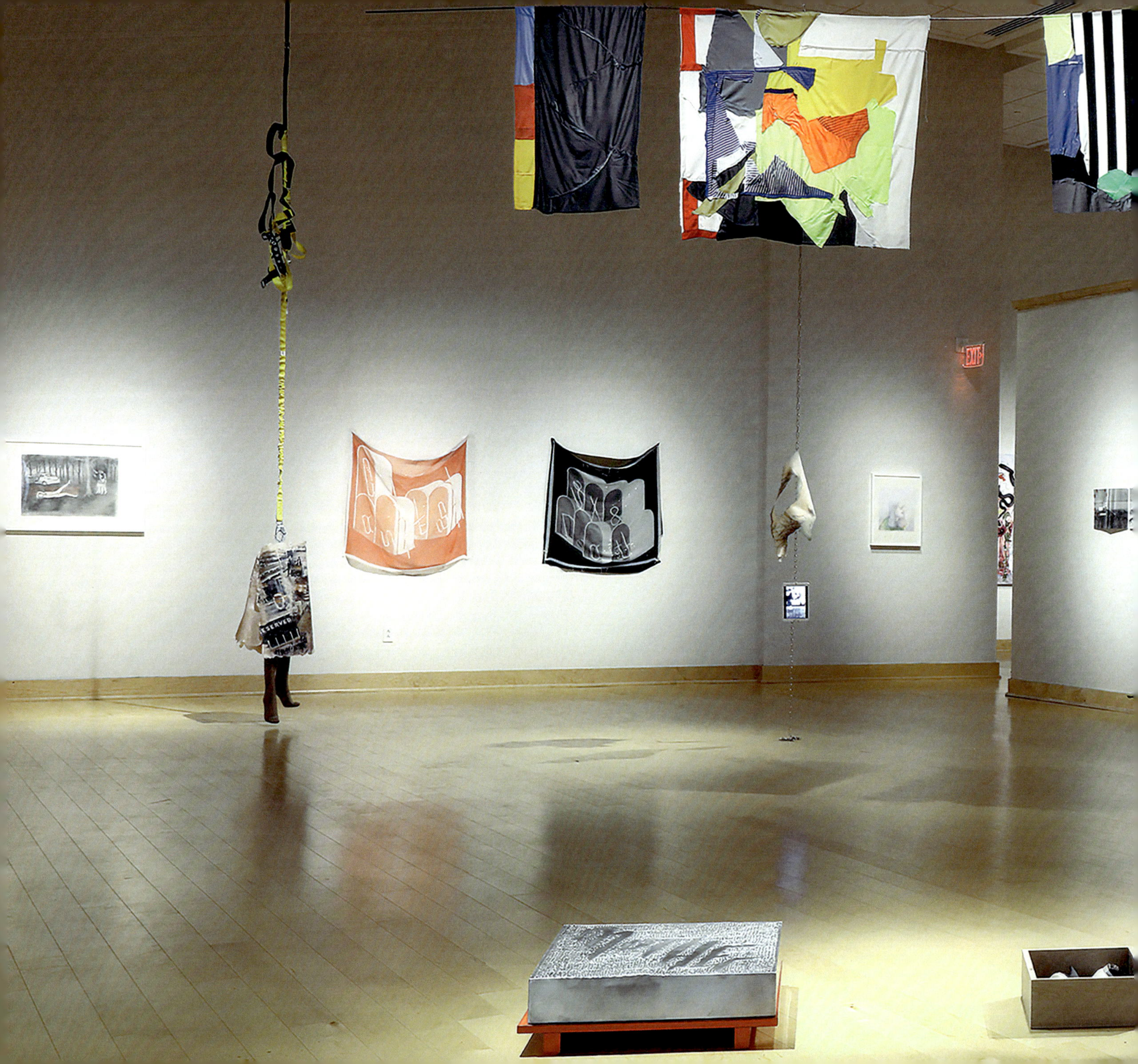
EXIT

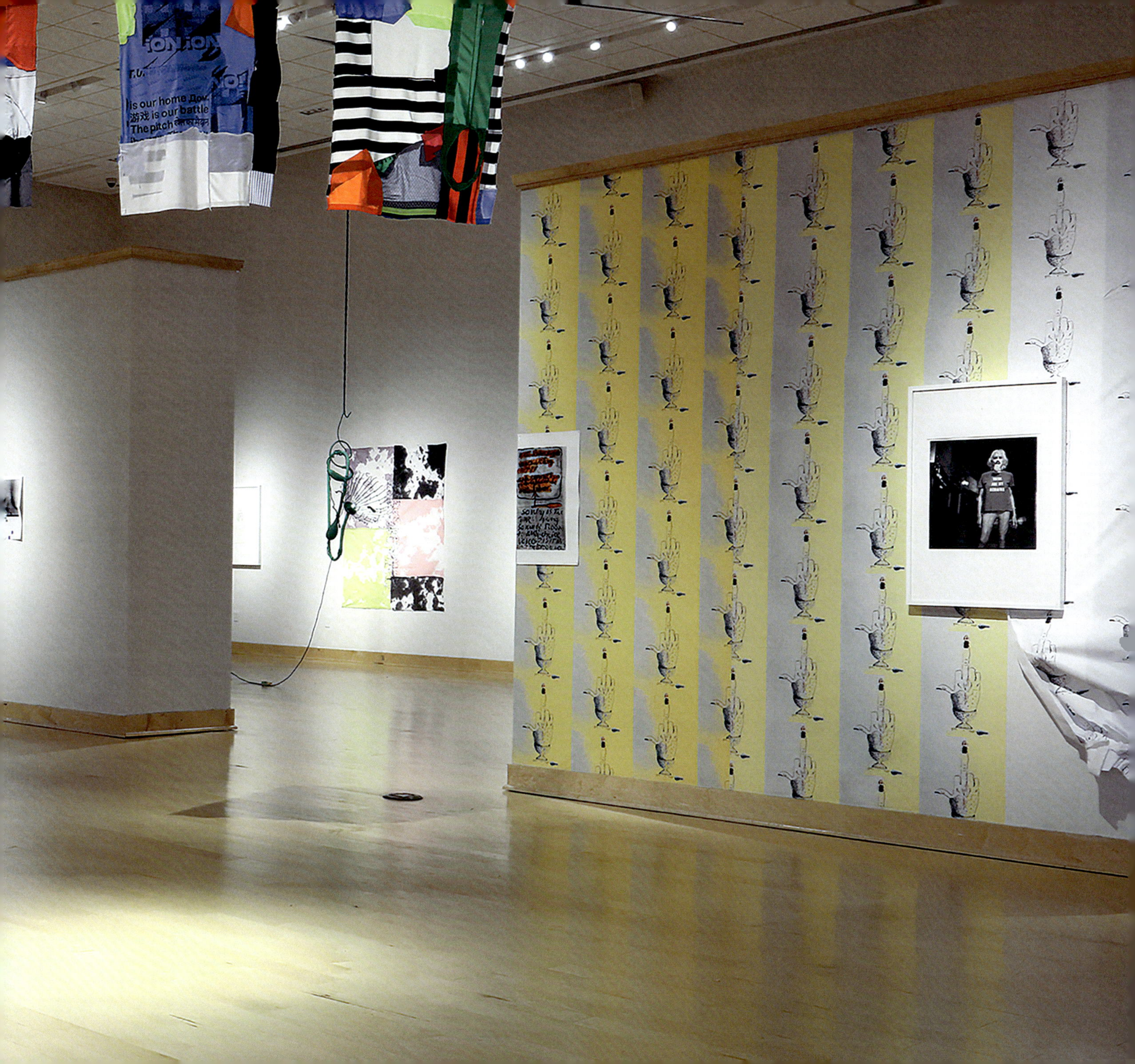
is our home
游戏 is our battle
The pitch

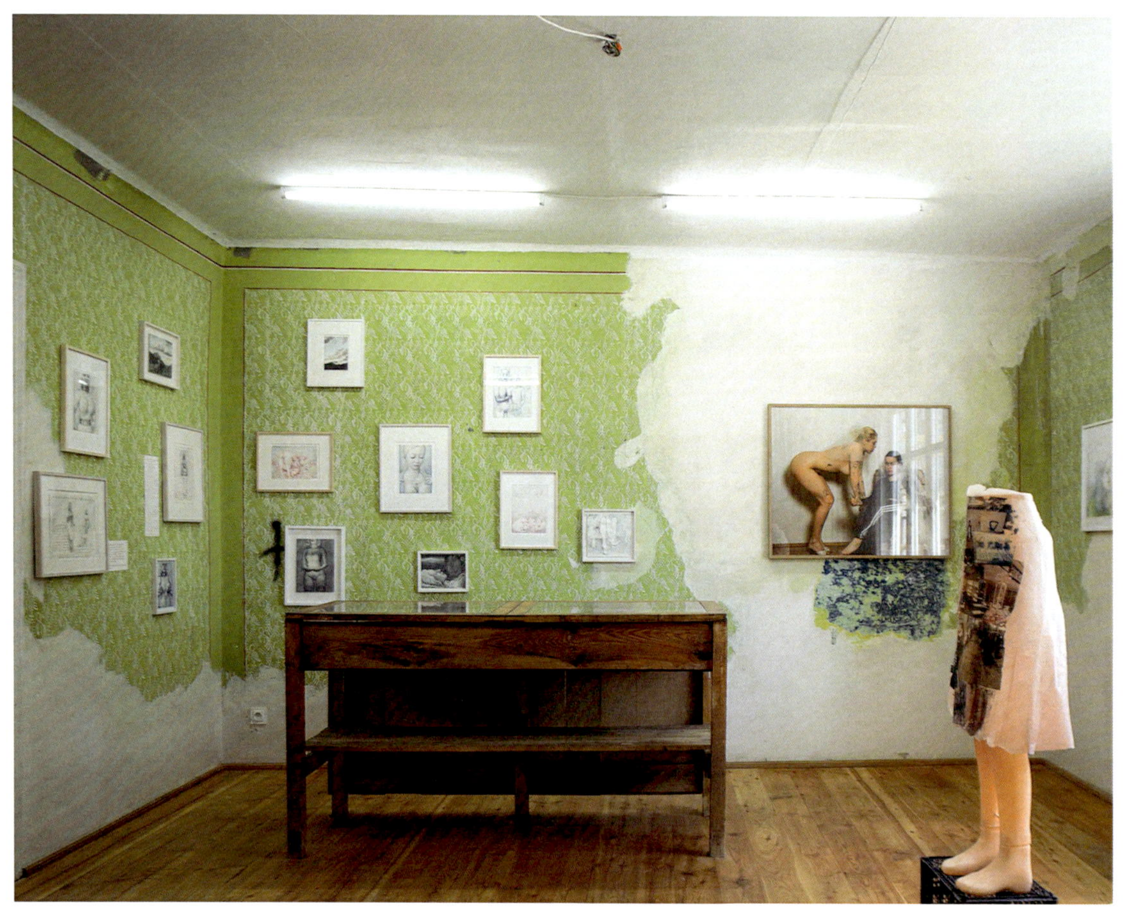

PREVIOUS Installation shot of *Girls + Eggs* at Duke Hall Gallery of Fine Art, 2024.
ABOVE Installation shot of *Girls + Eggs* at CU AT SADKA, Krakow, Poland, 2022.
OPPOSITE Installation shot of *Girls + Eggs* at The Art Gallery of the College of Staten Island, 2022.

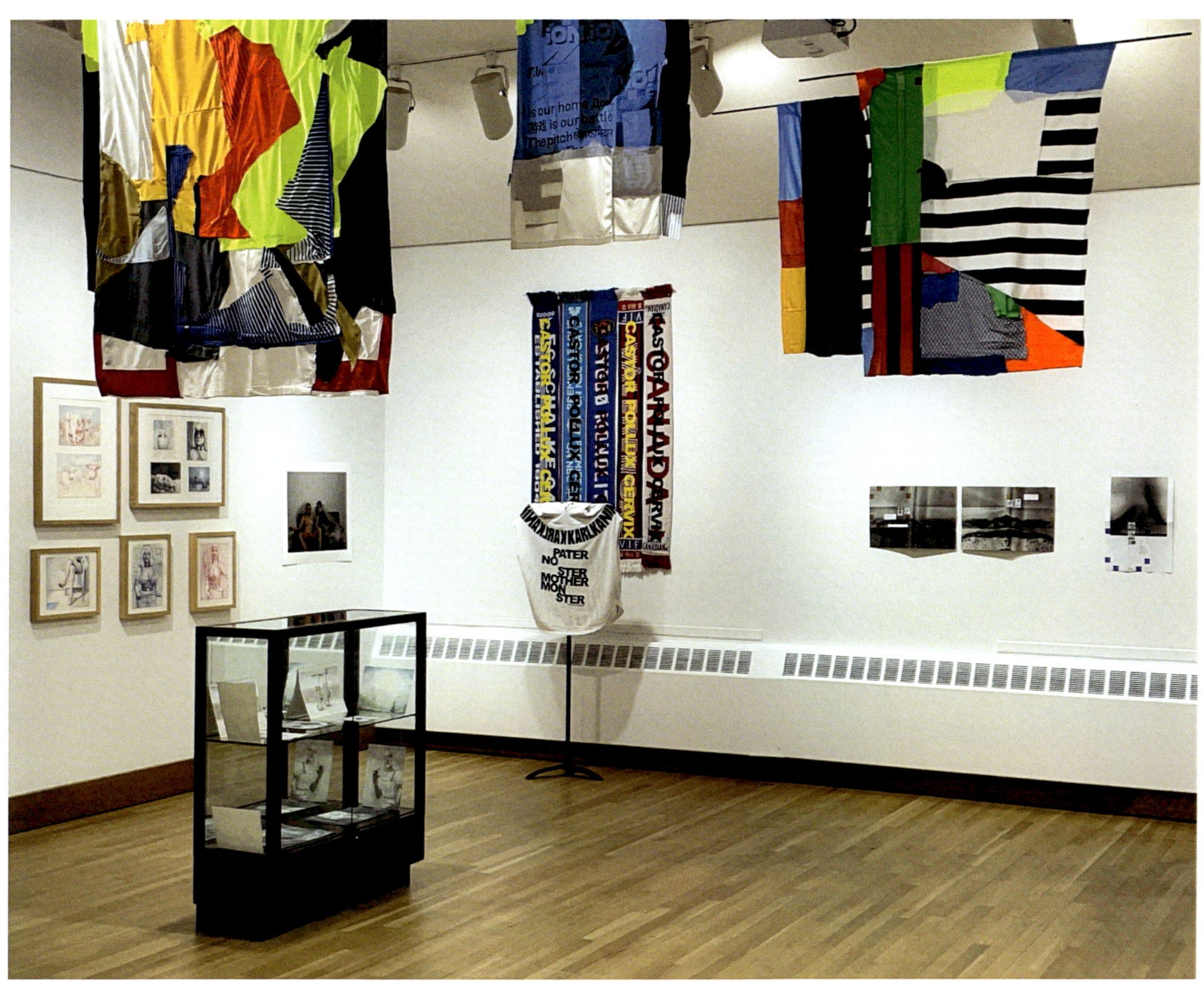
PATER
NO
STER
MOTHER
MON
STER

Curatorial Statement
Siona Wilson

Only some of the girls in this show have eggs, but we have all eaten them. Eggs – soft boiled, hard boiled, poached, deviled, scrambled, over-easy, sunny side up, coddled – lovely, golden, tasty, wholesome eggs. Eggs: *the socially acceptable abortion*.

Boy asks girl: how do you like your eggs in the morning?
Girl answers: *unfertilized*!!!

There's a girl in Texas on the run, chased by gun toting cowboys and cowgirls. This mob of Stetson-wearing vigilantes gallops after her, swinging lassos, kicking up dust, charging her down. Ready to corral. She's a container of precious eggs. Eggs from God. Eggs that must not be broken. Fuck the girl, protect the eggs!

There's a girl in Krakow heading for Berlin. Nauseous, she rides the Flixbus. The toilet is broken, her sickbag has split. She's a container of precious eggs. Eggs from God. Eggs that must not be broken. Fuck the girl, protect the eggs!

Girls + Eggs is an exhibition in alliance with all these outlaw girls. Girls on the run. Girls who have run out of eggs. Girls with runny eggs.

Some of the eggs have migrated. Some of the girls were once boys. Some of the girls are still boys. Boys with mutated egg sacks. Testes are overcooked ovaries. Their eggs failed, fallen, dropped off the wall, like Humpty Dumpty. Oh dear! Whoopsie daisy!

C U at Sadka! An exhibition in a house, in a garden, in the suburbs of Krakow comes to the Shenandoah Valley in the Commonwealth of Virginia (by way of Staten Island, New York).

~Siona Wilson, Curator
(All her eggs are cooked)

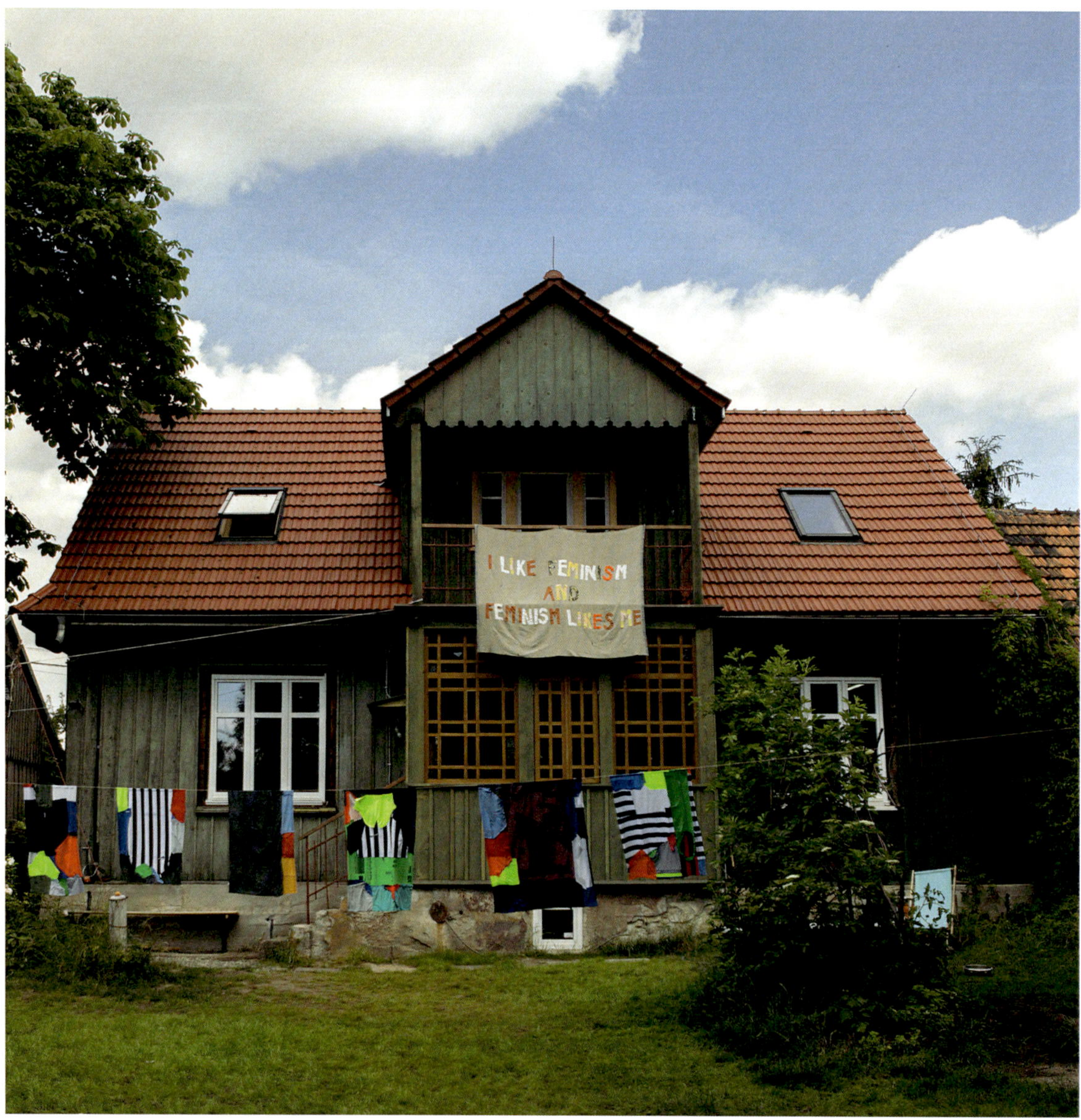

Installation shot of *Girls + Eggs* at CU AT SADKA, Krakow, Poland, 2022.

Introduction

Laughing Hysterically: Feminist Curating in Dark Times

by Siona Wilson

Girls + Eggs is a ridiculous title. Hysterical laughter is sometimes the only response when women have been rendered incapable of making decisions about their bodies and lives, when the police detain and interrogate girls after experiencing miscarriages, when doctors dare not treat dangerous ectopic pregnancies in case a politicized court decides that "risk to life" was not yet met, and underage pregnant rape victims are forced to give birth or prosecuted for seeking an abortion elsewhere. All of this, when the US still has no mandatory maternity leave, politicians prop up a for-profit healthcare system in utter chaos, Black and Hispanic women are four times more likely than white women to die in childbirth, and huge numbers of the sick are bankrupted by medical debt. So, we laughed a lot when the idea of the exhibition first came about in the early hours of the morning after a long night of fun. But our laughter was driven by rage. This was the summer of 2021. I visited Krakow as part of my first overseas travels since the lonely months of the pandemic. Agnieszka Szostek and Michael Biber, who I knew from time I spent in Berlin, moved to Krakow in 2020 (a return home for Szostek, Biber is German). They bought a rundown traditional wooden country house in the suburbs of the city. It's called Sadka. This is the name of the street, but naming the house was also a kind of christening, giving her subjectivity, identity, and a new life.

Sadka was a weekend getaway that would double as an occasional exhibition space. In August of 2021, a month or so before the first exhibition in the house (titled, *PPS: it's a progressive fantasy (...)*), the upstairs bedrooms were finished with new pine panels and downstairs was only lightly renovated with the torn and graffitied old-fashioned wallpaper remaining as a record of generations past. One room with wild floral walls has the spraypainted letters "TV" written in the corner like the notes of a delinquent interior decorator (see p. 31). At this time, Sadka had electric lighting but no functioning plumbing, so we peed in the garden and decamped to the city apartment the next day.

Before this visit, I was only vaguely aware of the mass demonstrations in numerous Polish cities protesting the new (old world) laws from 2020 prohibiting abortion in almost every case. The Human Rights Watch

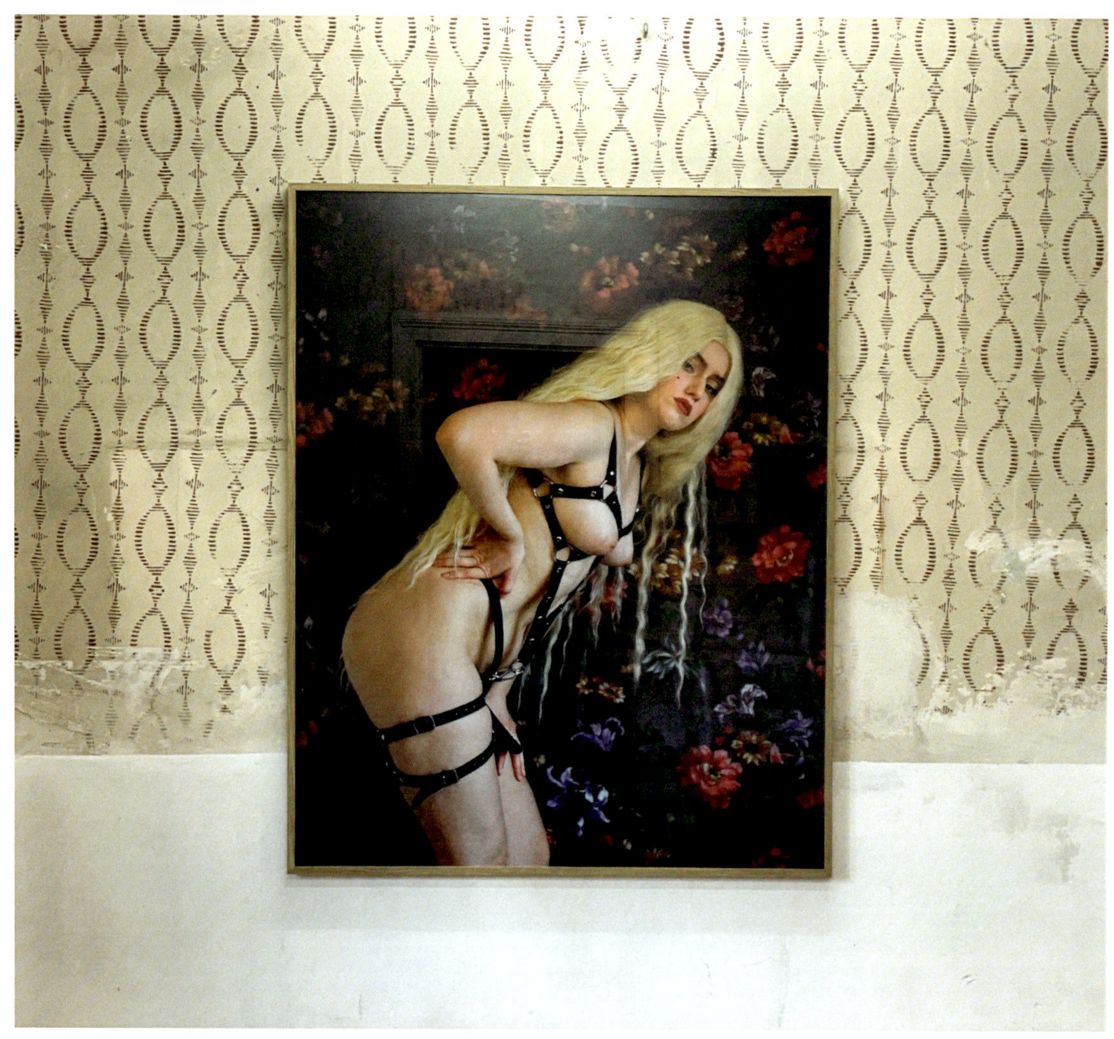

Maria Kniaginin-Ciszewska *Prezent (Gift)*, 2021, C-print, shown at CU AT SADKA.

report on the state and church directed witch hunts against Polish women were published in 2023, but anecdotal accounts circulated on social media.[1] In Berlin, there was also some talk about this since Polish women were traveling across the border to access German health care. It seemed like time was moving in reverse. Soon after, the first rumors that the US supreme court might overturn the federal abortion law, so-called "Roe versus Wade," were reported. But the return to pre-feminist values was already well established in the US. I made a drawing, a curatorial meditation, that I turned into a Warholesque wallpaper design at Duke Hall (see. p. 23). Laughing hysterically, the middle finger of a woman's hand bursts out of a boiled egg, as a feminist "fuck you" to the ridiculous logic of these dark times.

Despite the election of Trump, most Poles I spoke to saw the US as the home of progressive politics. Many families had relatives who had migrated to the US, often during communist times. For them, it was a place where the repressions of the old world (the Catholic church and Communist party) held no sway, or so they thought. Perhaps this was once partly true, but a new nasty conservatism is running rampant. We're living in a new old world, cynically celebrating its own criminal hypocrisy.

Girls + Eggs, the juxtaposition of ideas and the bringing together of works, captures our hysterical rage. I was an economy class travelling curator with an exhibition in a suitcase. Literally, the works from the US were packed into my luggage. Although some things were printed on site and others were sent in the mail, the first two iterations of *Girls + Eggs* involved a lot of heavy bags. Hospitality was also part of the process. The labor of curating this show, like the ideas explored in the artists' works, was embedded in the practicalities of living, caring, and being together. In doing so, we expressed solidarity across borders of nation, region, gender, sex, sexuality, and age.

Women, men, transgender, non-binary, queer, lesbian, cis-gender, mothers, perverts, fathers, child-free, dog lovers, and feminists, *Girls + Eggs* stages a world of individuals, characters, thoughts, and fragments from those repressed by and resisting the return to old world patriarchal norms. The works, artists, and exhibition venues contribute to the affective landscape of the project. Sadka, the birth venue, first old-fashioned mother for our *Girls + Eggs*, functioned almost like another artist. She provided the anchor to place, land, domesticity, religion, and tradition. I was a curator in residence for the duration of the exhibition in June 2022. I slept in a bed-

1 "Poland: Abortion Witch Hunt Targets Women, Doctors" Human Rights Watch, September 14, 2023. Accessed, January 15, 2024: https://www.hrw.org/news/2023/09/14/poland-abortion-witch-hunt-targets-women-doctors#:~:text=Cases%20that%20Human%20Rights%20Watch,eliminated%20legal%20abortion%20in%20Poland.

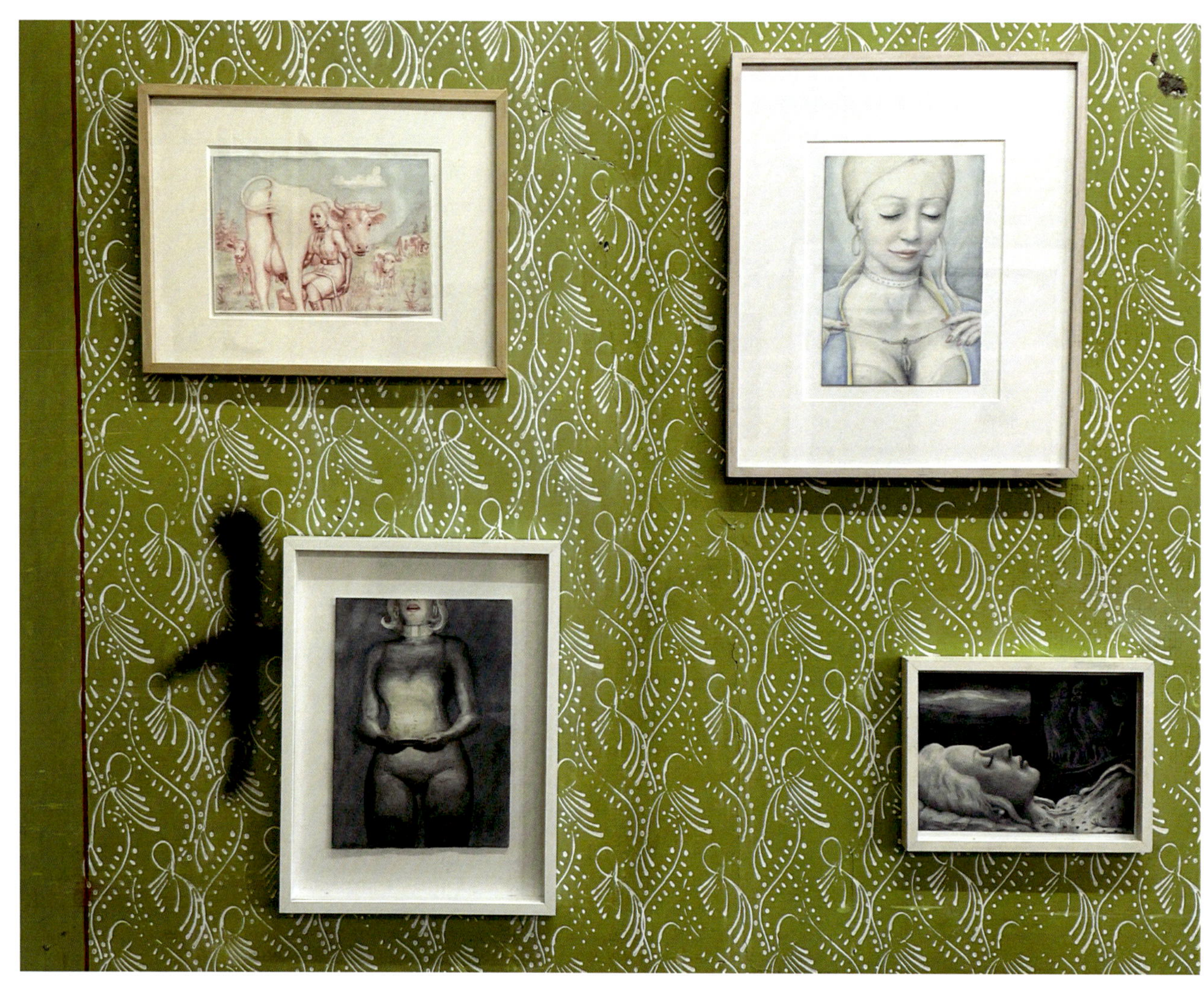

OPPOSITE Kozlov *Papieżyca (Popetress)*, 2021, Digital print of painting, 5.5 x 8.5 inches.
ABOVE Installation shot showing various works by Piotr Dłużniewski, CU AT SADKA, 2022.

room upstairs and offered visitors tea (beer or vodka) when they came over to see the show. Like the elderly, conservative population that supported the Polish return to patriarchal values, Sadka was our grandmother muse.

When *Girls + Eggs* came to Staten Island, I saw this as a geographical parallel to Poland. Staten Island is to New York City as Poland is to Europe: they each belong to a larger geopolitical body, yet they are geographically, socially, and psychically peripheral. Both are less accepting of difference, more politically conservative, and officially supportive of the rollback on women's right to choose. Each place also includes powerful voices of opposition, inclusion, and advocacy. Traveling south to Virginia, a historic region in the (old) new world, is—perhaps desperately—a kind of hopeful parallel for future change. Despite the shared conservativism, Poland has since voted out the political right and voters in Virginia refused to change the abortion laws in elections in 2023. But there's still plenty for feminists to laugh about, hysterically.

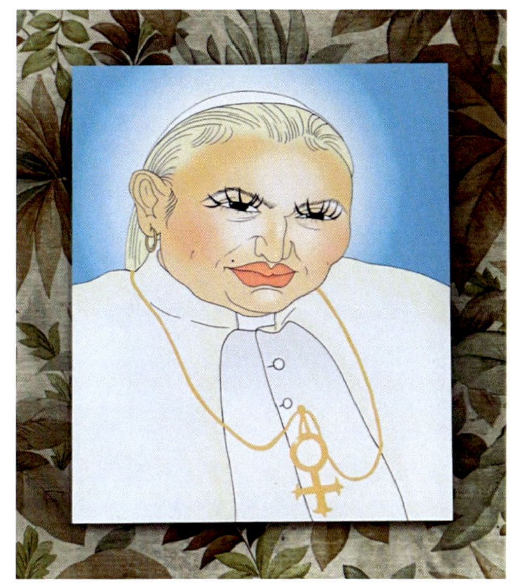

I approached the curation of this exhibition affectively. Reproductive justice, the right to choose, to have sovereignty over our bodies, is embedded in a much broader political, cultural, and emotional landscape of sexual citizenship. *Girls + Eggs* animates this broader arena of feeling and living. There are only a few works in this exhibition that directly reference the issue of reproductive justice and the symbol of the egg. The 80-year-old LA-based transgender artist, Pippa Garner, is one example. The slogan tee-shirts presented on her aging body read, "If you knock me up, I'll knock you down," and "these are my remains." Her photographs show performances from everyday life, from life lived as embodied performativity, laughing hysterically at

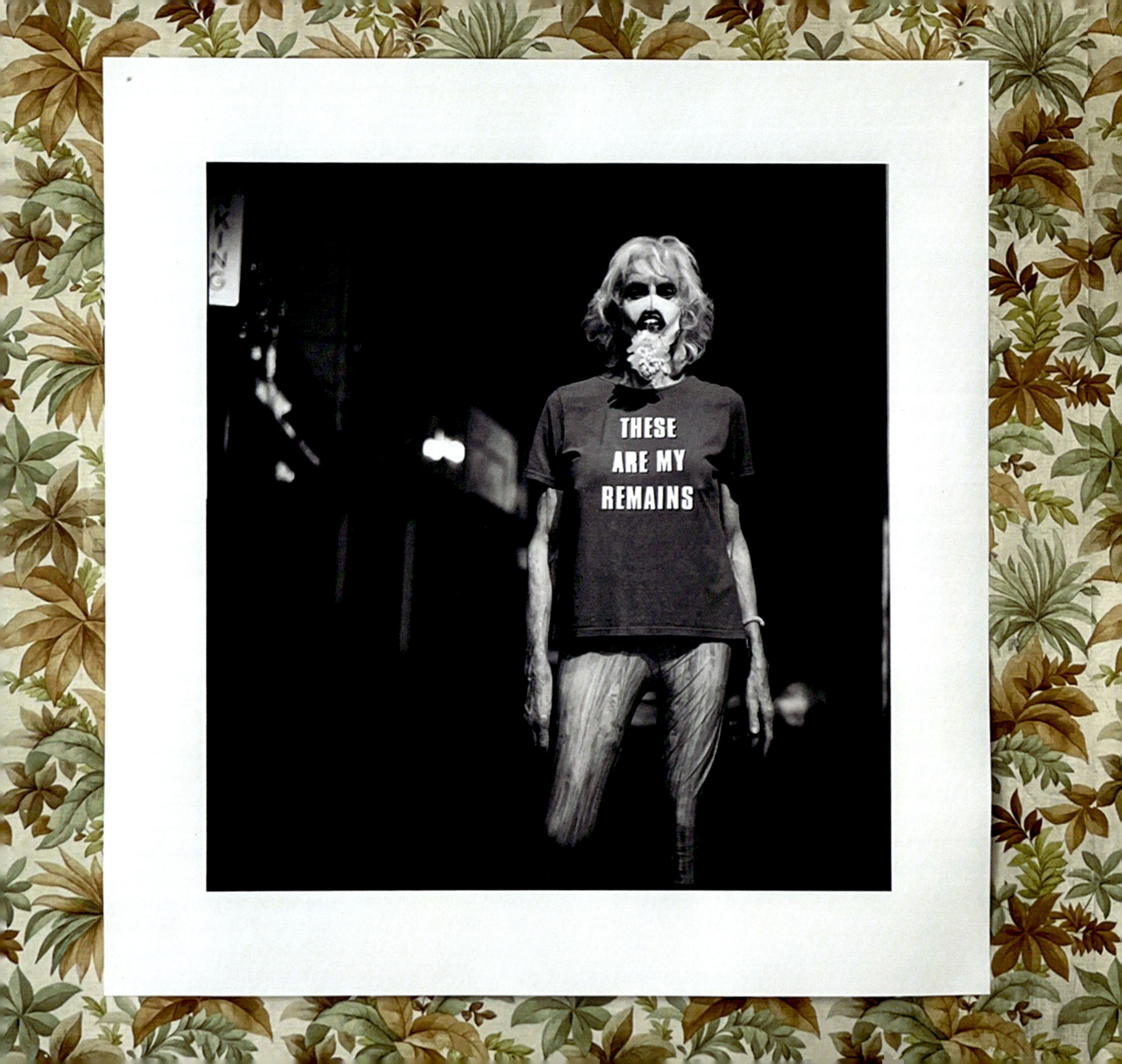
THESE
ARE MY
REMAINS

the cis-gender ideals of heterosexual reproduction and taboos about a body aging. Peter Kunt, Piotr Dłużniewski, and Martyna Borowiecka each made egg-themed works in response to the acidic tone of camp carnivalesque expressed in my curatorial statement. The second version of the show, at the Art Gallery of the College of Staten Island, included Beatrix Reinhardt's *Untitled* (2022) (see page 41 and 43), that used eggshells as miniature plant pots to grow weeds she had propagated from sidewalk cracks and local parks. Egg cartons and an ostrich egg also appear in photographs featuring African models. While these works, made during a residency in South Africa, were about being out of place not reproductive justice, Reinhardt was happy to plant her ideas amidst the girls in our show.

Other works approach the topic indirectly. Biber's *Flags on a Line*, installed on a washing line in the garden of Sadka, evoke domestic gendered labor, protest, and confused nationalism, but the fabric, offcuts of soccer jerseys, is archetypically masculine, macho even. The tradition of geometric abstraction here occupies the site and materials of other social spaces (see p. 33). At the same time, this work connects with Sonia Delaunay and Sophie Taeuber Arp's early abstract quilts, evoking the repressed feminine within the history of modernist art.

Maria Kniaginin-Ciszewska's large-scale erotic photographs of herself and her female lover present tableau images of the kinky queer couple as part of Polish everyday life. Against the traditional walls of Sadka, these images felt even more provocative (see p. 14). Home is as much a site of repression and violence as it is a place of comfort and safety. Monika Drożyńska's embroidery works animate and parody the contradictions within traditional domesticity. Evoking the widely held anti-immigrant feeling in Poland, notions of home, of belonging are cut through with the inverse (see p. 34). Her video animation, *American Dream is Dream*, references the racist treatment of Poles in the US, along with other "white" ethnic groups, suggesting a cycle of victim to oppressor. Madeline Kuzak's intricate pencil drawing, *Bowers of Bliss*, offers a shard of collective female cruelty, a fragment of a dark narrative in which women violently persecute other women (see p. 22). The politics of reproductive justice includes women on both sides of the issue.

Kuzak and Kniaginin-Ciszewska are early career artists, but their work sits amongst contributions from established feminist figures. Moyra Davey printed some old negatives dating from her art school years in the 1980s. As another echo of domestic norms, these three images arrived in the mail at Sadka folded into self-made envelopes. As with other photographic works by Davey, the postage and address labels are a visible part of the

OPPOSITE Pippa Garner *These are my Remains*, 2021, Digital Print (photograph by Reynaldo Rivera), 24 x 26 inches.

surface of the images when presented unfolded and simply pinned to the gallery wall. The modest materiality and quiet imagery contrasts with the "stilt coupled with bloat," associated with the staged scenes and high production values of museum-ready large-scale tableau form photography.[2] Mira Schor, an original member of Judy Chicago and Miriam Schapiro's Feminist Art Program at CalArts in Los Angeles and participant in its landmark exhibition, *Womanhouse* (1972), contributed facsimiles of her Instagram series *New York Times Intervention* (see pp. 28 and 36). Schor's habit of reading the morning paper became a studio practice of enraged feminist graffiti. Begun after the election of Trump, these crude edits scrawled directly on to the physical newspaper were made in response to the anodyne commentary of the *New York Times*. These works operate on the walls of the exhibition space as something like the screaming signage pasted in the First International Dada Fair in Berlin in 1920 (see p. 34).

Szosek's *Untitled (War doesn't mean the End of Fashion. Sanctions on Russia are the Inspiration)*, a latex A-line skirt imprinted with a collage of commercial imagery from communist era Poland and present-day luxury stores, was made in response to the war in Ukraine (see p. 53). Another echo of the Dada fair (the *ur*-form for avant-garde protest exhibitions), in the use of a display manikin, "the bitch," as she was fondly known, became an uncanny resident of Sadka. Both object and space combine the old world and new, this, and Szostek's other latex works are like diseased skin with a hint of the fetishistic. Kat Chamberlin's chiffon prints, framed loosely with clean, tight vinyl echo with Szostek's works. Her cryptic micro poems, *Sex and Death* and *Gash on a Lash*, operate like a cypher or an unknown alphabet, since they are not easily readable (see p. 38).

As with Chamberlin and Szostek, materials—in this case, found materials—are eloquent with condensed

2 Moyra Davey, "Notes on Photography & Accident." *Long Life Cool White: Photographs and Essays by Moyra Davey* (2008), 2.

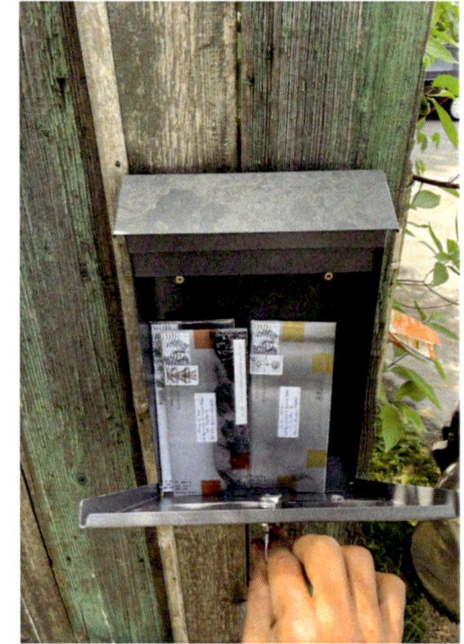

Documentation showing the arrival of Moyra Davey's work at CU AT SADKA.

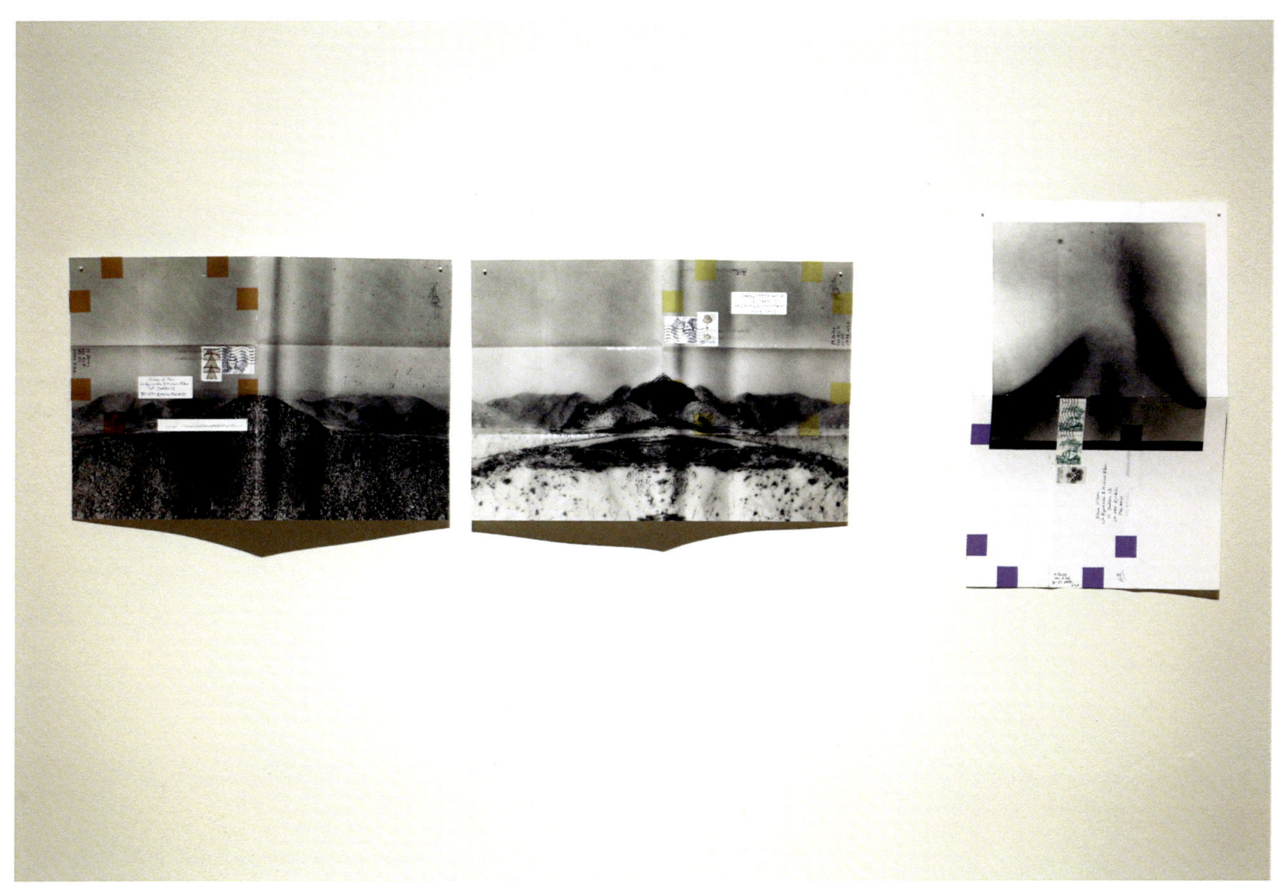

Moyra Davey, Mirrored Landscapes (*Triptych*), 2022, 3 c-prints, tape, postage, ink; courtesy of the artist; Greengrassi, London; and Galerie Buchholz, Berlin/Cologne/New York.

references in the sculpture of Danni O'Brien. Together with Maja Krysiak, O'Brien is a new addition to the Duke Hall Gallery version of *Girls + Eggs*. A graduate of the BFA program at JMU, O'Brien mobilizes a sinister eroticism that combines the gynecologist's office with the used bookstore and the kitchen pantry (see p. 26-7). While O'Brien's sculptures are fragile and precarious in their congregated arrangements, Krysiak's free-hanging cloth painting draws on the representational language of violent gendered mythology (see p. 29). Her depiction of the diminutive female held in the palm of a monstrous giant is an old-world reference that seems ever new.

From the transgressive excitement of Kniaginin-Ciszewska and Dłużniewski's erotic works to the blazing fury of Schor's protest scrawls, the affective mood shifts down gear with other more contemplative works. Oskar Korsár's intense series of portrait drawings of imaginary figures—female and gender queer—seem lost in interior thought. Interspersed amongst the other works, these pensive characters operate as avatars for the many pregnant girls—past, present, and future—nauseous, riding the flixbus to Berlin, where Korsár lives (see p. 48). They might also evoke the somber disquiet of the desperate girls travelling across the US to find an abortion providing state.

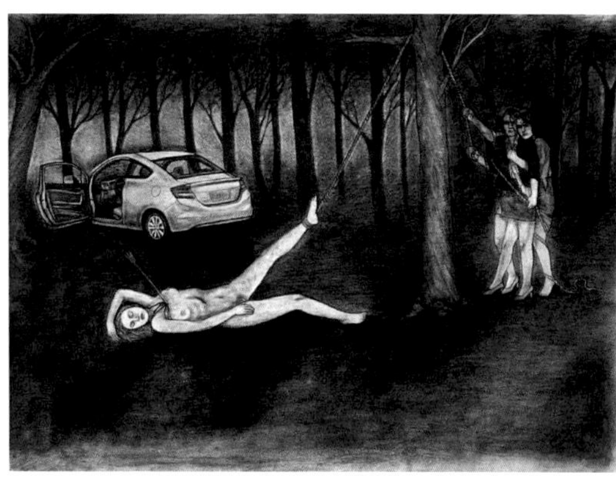

Madeline Kuzak *Bower of Bliss*, 2020, pencil on paper, 24 x 18 inches.

The mythic is domesticated in Arobal's *Self Portrait Pregnant* and Magda Buczek's *Castor, Pollux, Cervix*. Waving the soccer scarf, for Castor and Pollux, children of rape, born from an egg, no cervix in site, turns the disavowal of the feminine into the collective chant (see p. 26-7). Arobal's tender image of the reproductive body as queer exists alongside works that assert the suppression of the maternal (a longstanding theme in western art). Greek mythology, with narratives of rape and violence, also expresses the masculine desire for autogenesis (see p. 48).

The affective curating at work in *Girls + Eggs* positions motherhood within a complex field of meaning and feeling. The strong feelings elicited by the backward shift in political culture are the kind that propel action, protest, and strong expressive assertions. But the issue

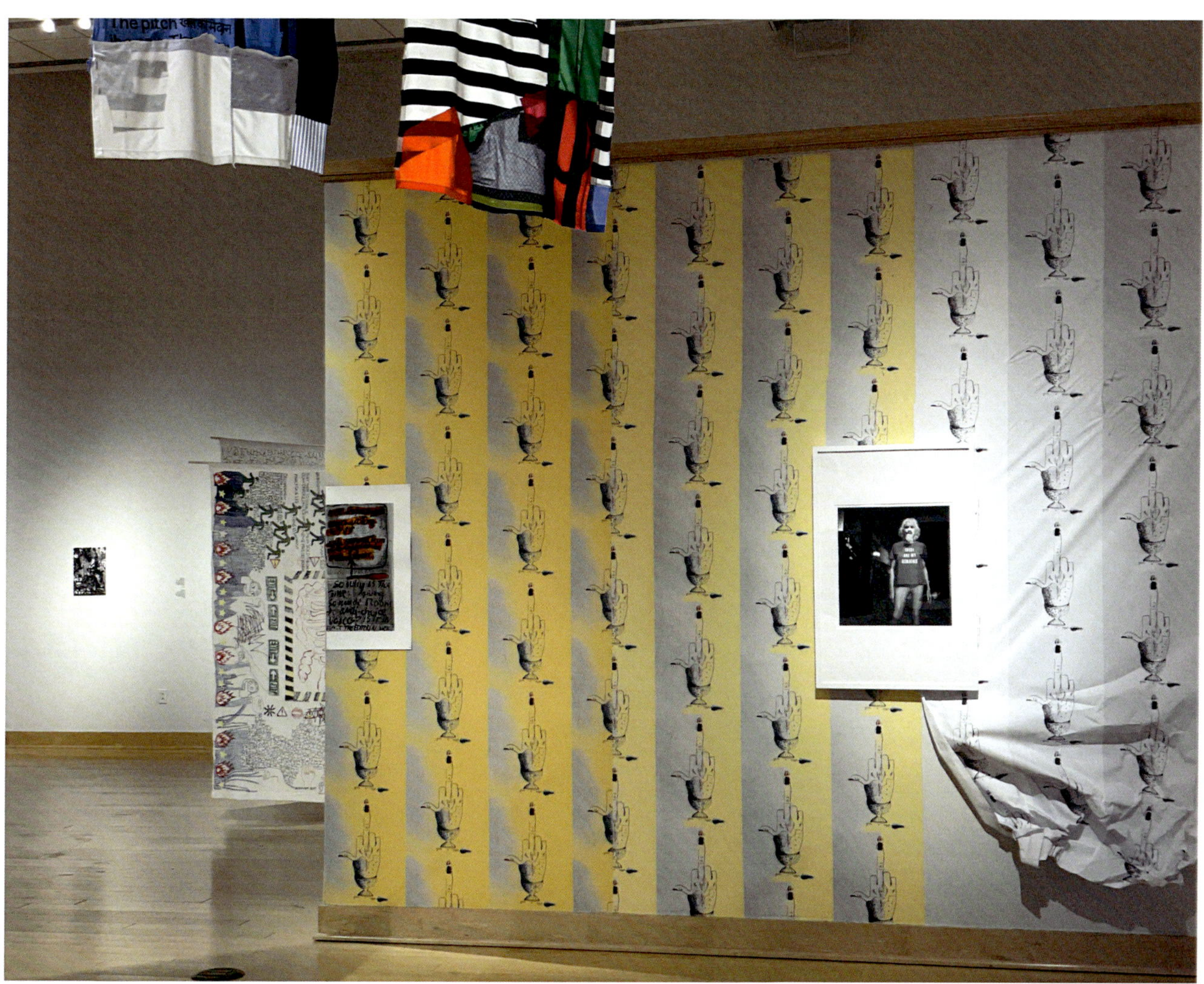

Installation shot of *Girls + Eggs* at Duke Hall Gallery of Fine Art, 2024.

of legal prohibition extends into other affective territories and connects to other forms of repression of sexual citizenship. Whose bodies count? Which bodies are permitted to exist and where? The picture we used for the cover of this book, Kat Chamberlin's *Image to Stand on*, suggests the denigration that underpins a politics of forced maternity. The menopausal curator stands on the carved aluminum depiction of the word "mother" rendered in a font that evokes punk. Yet mothers, the artist as mother, all the failed mothers, the refusal to mother, motherhood as part of the cultural sourcebook of artistic expression, the ~~mother~~ is still under erasure. She is usually limited to a very narrow affective range that oscillates between sentimentality and embarrassment. The mother is either elevated and emptied out of complexity or denigrated as beneath consideration.

She is a fart in the chapel of art.

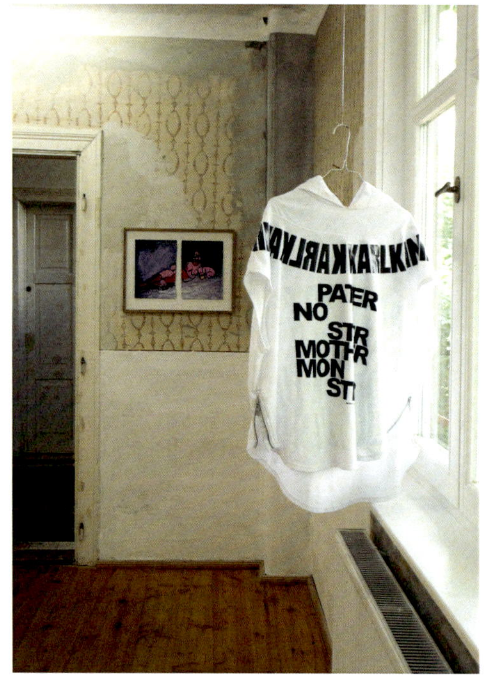

Installation shot of *Girls + Eggs* at C U AT SADKA, with Magda Buczek, *Greetings from the Strange Hotel*, 2022, paint, molotov and markers on found paper

FOREGROUND
Magda Buczek, *PATER NOSTER MOTHER MONSTER*, 2022, upcycled jersey with printed text.

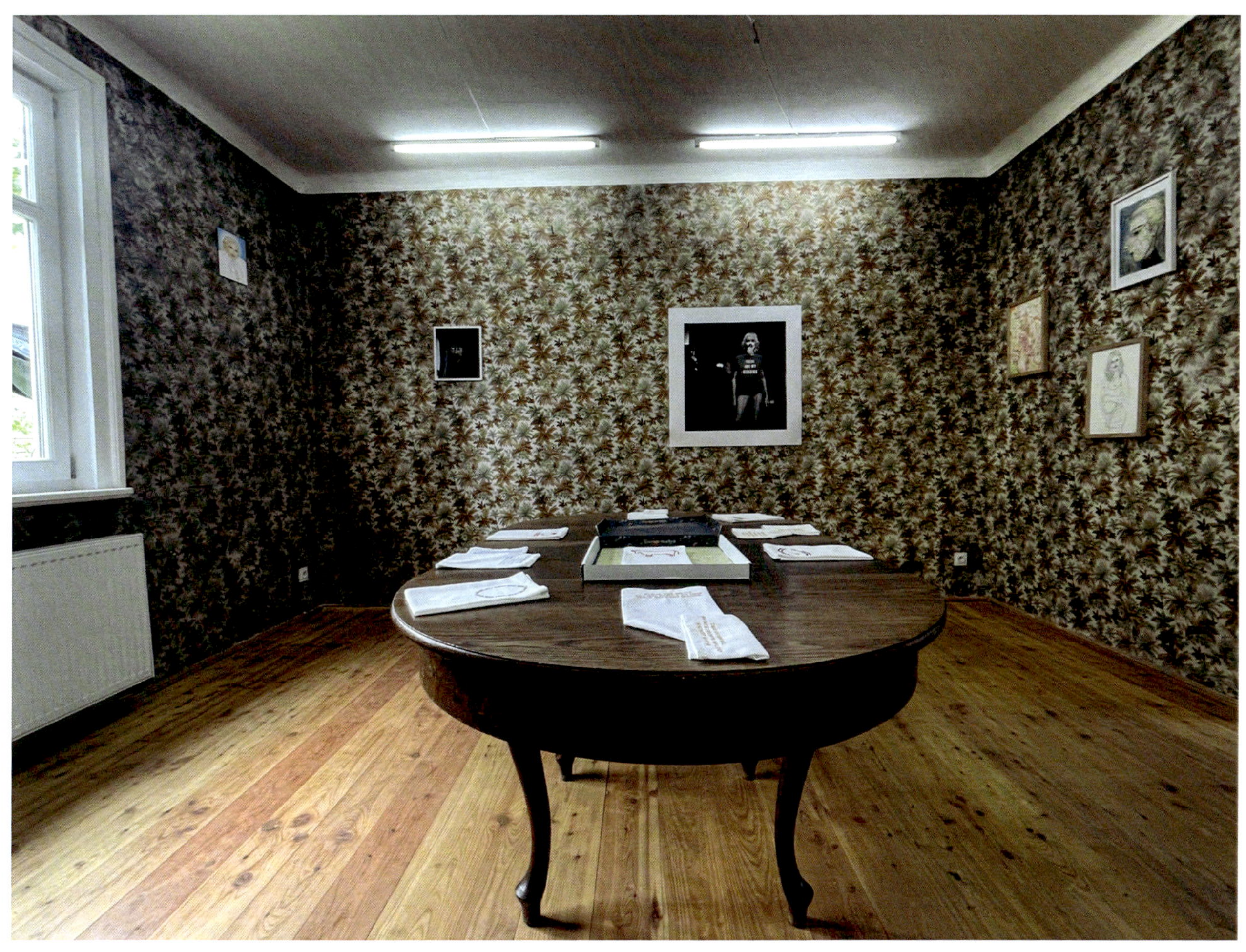

Installation shot of *Girls + Eggs* at CU AT SADKA, Krakow, Poland, 2022.

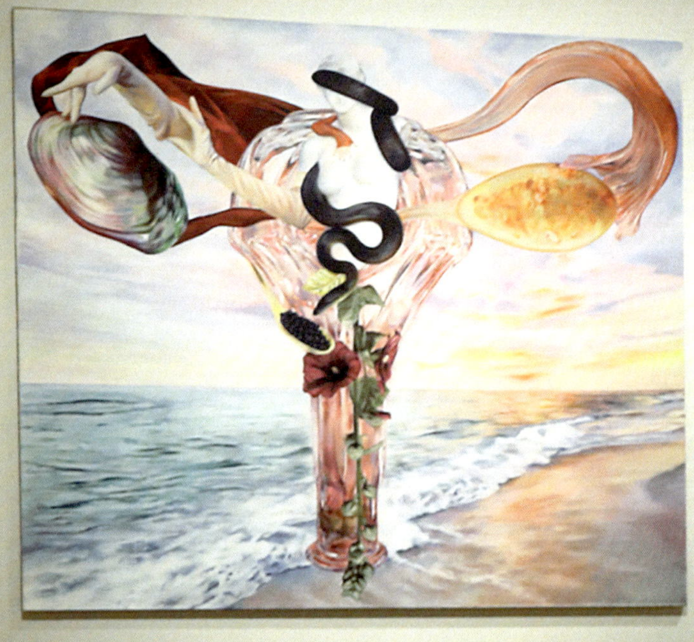

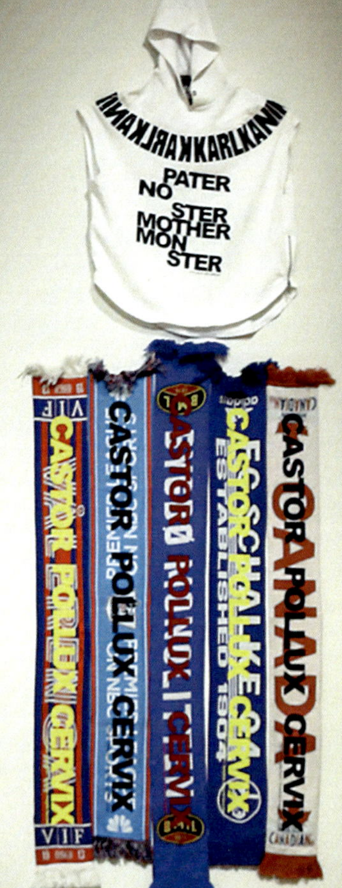
PATER
NO
STER
MOTHER
MON
STER
CASTOR POLLUX CERVIX
CASTOR POLLUX CERVIX
CASTOR POLLUX CERVIX
CASTOR POLLUX CERVIX
ESTABLISHED 1904
CASTOR POLLUX CERVIX
CANADA

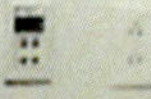

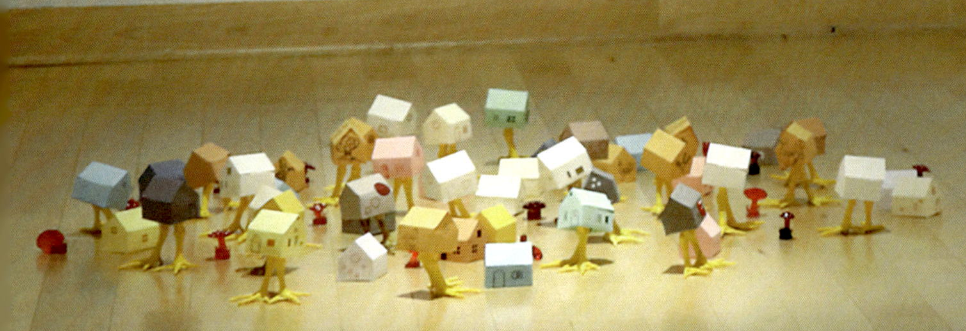

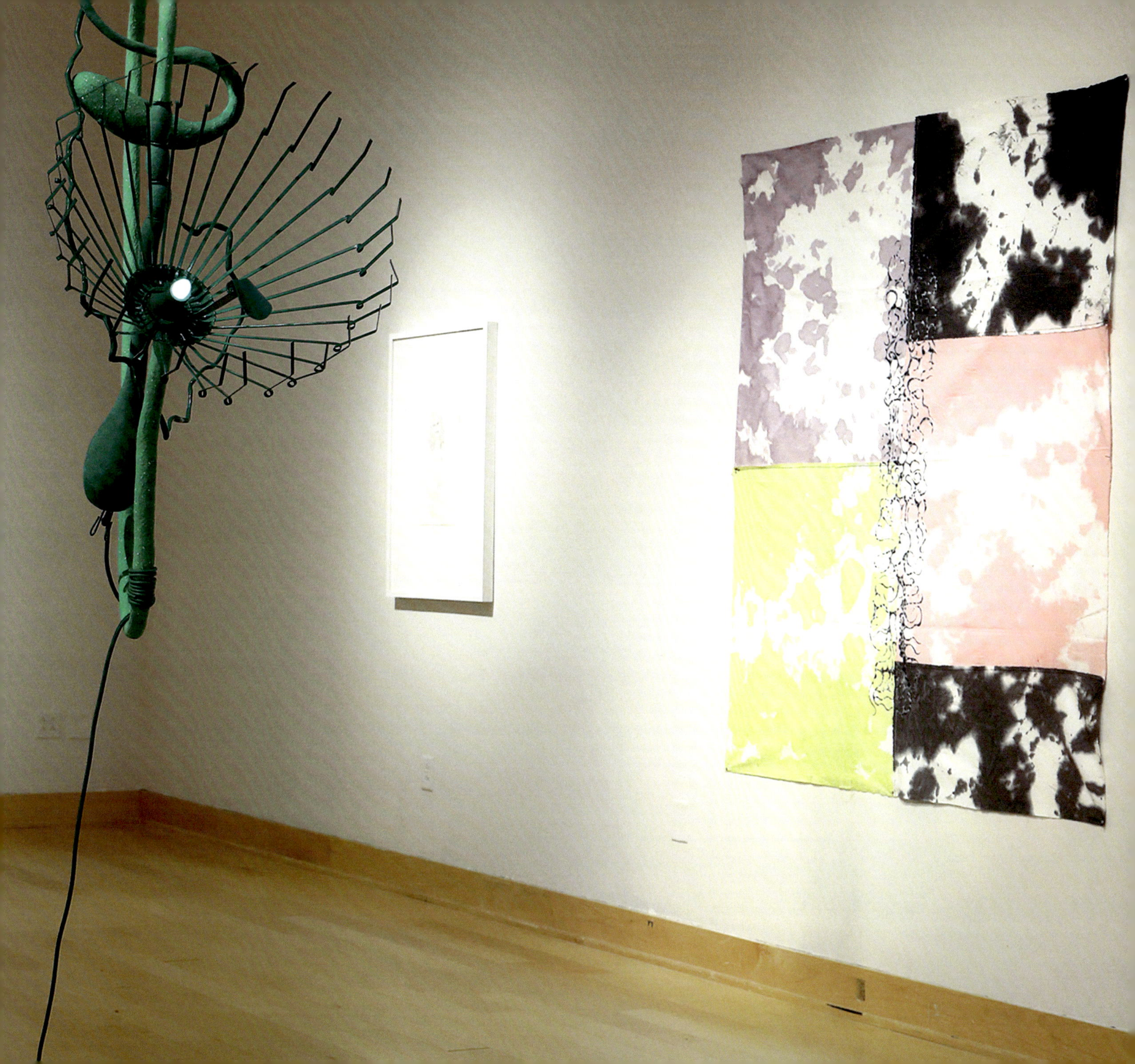

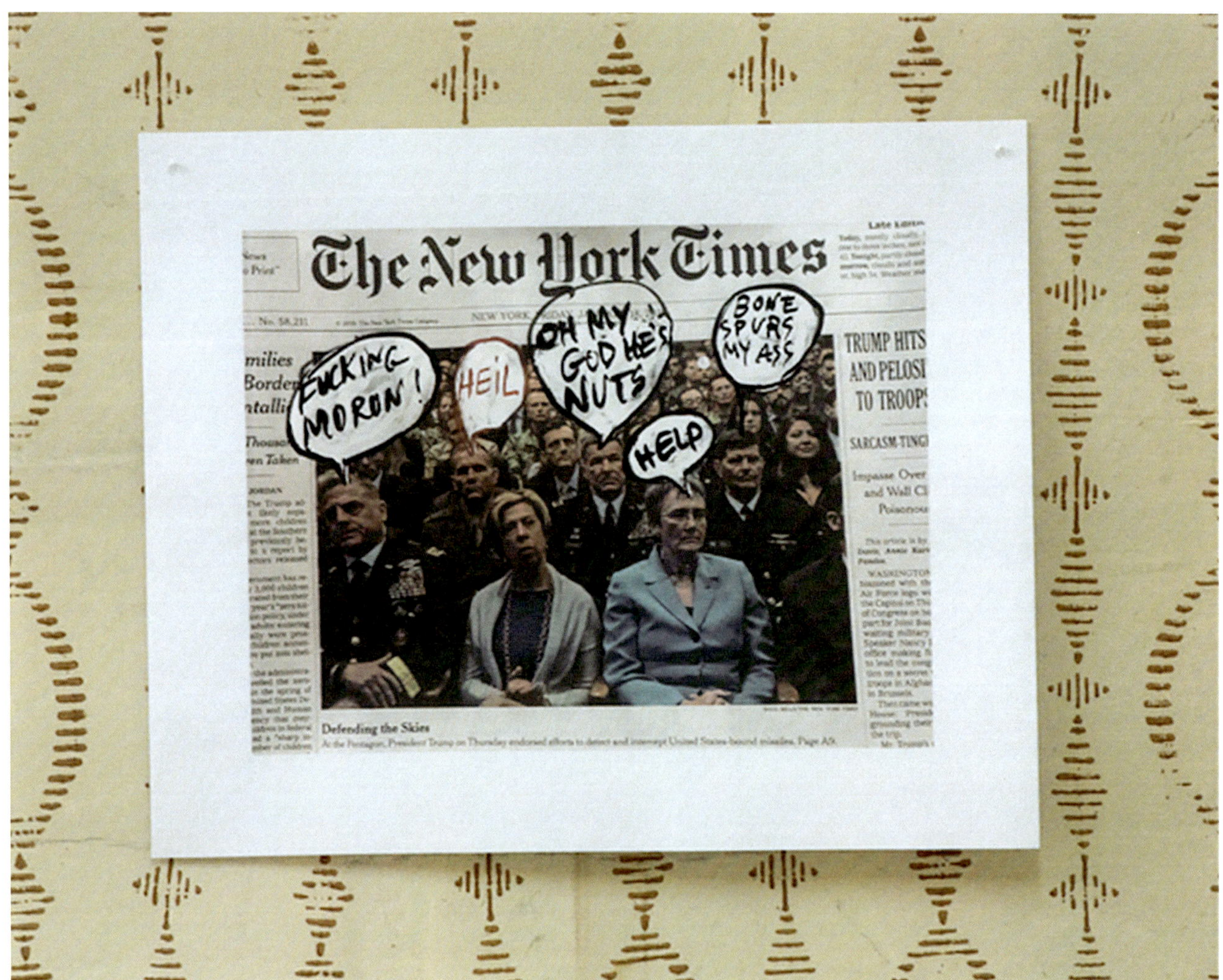

The New York Times
FUCKING MORON!
HEIL
OH MY GOD HE'S NUTS
BONE SPURS MY ASS
HELP
TRUMP HITS
AND PELOSI
Defending the Skies
At the Pentagon, President Trump on Thursday endorsed efforts to detect and intercept United States-bound missiles. Page A9.

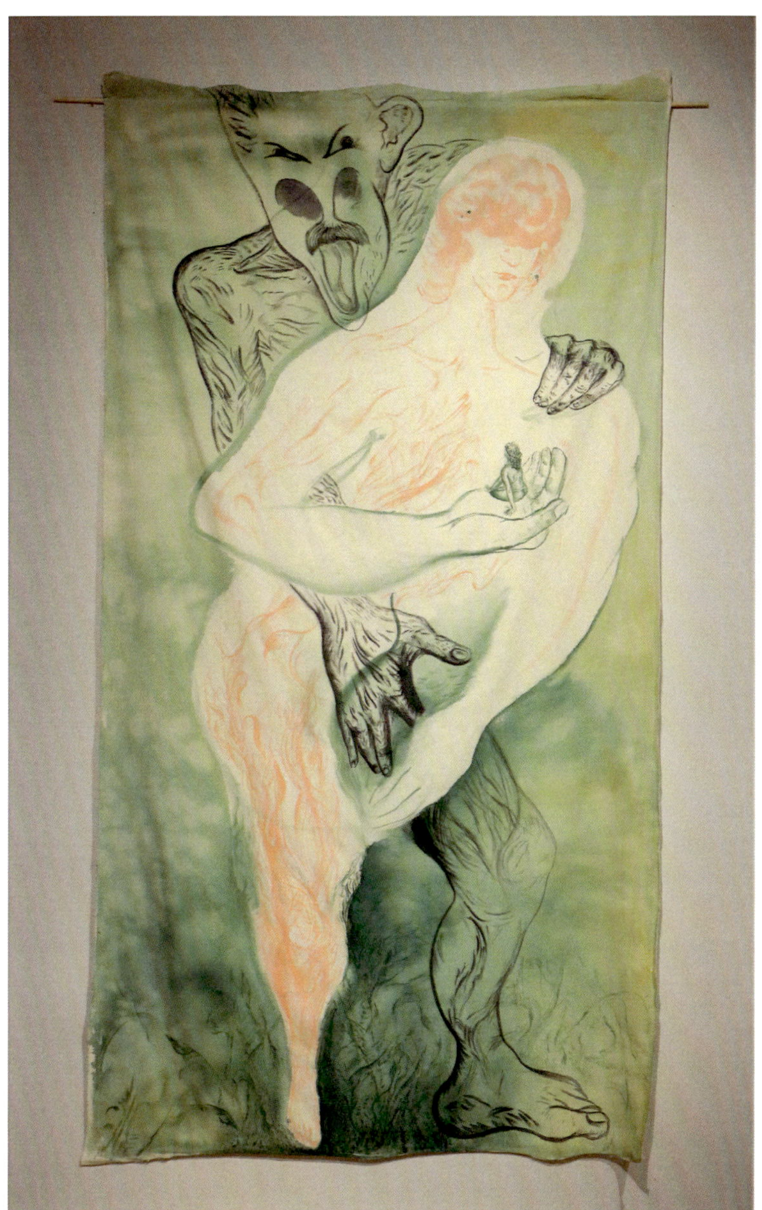

PREVIOUS
Installation shot of *Girls + Eggs* at Duke Hall Gallery of Fine Art, 2024.

OPPOSITE
Mira Schor "Fucking Moron," from *New York Time Intervention*, 2019-23, facsimile print, ink on New York Times, 16 x 19 inches.

CURRENT
Maja Krysiak *Body #8* from *Headless Giantesses* Series, 2023, silk paint on cotton, 63 x 118.5 inches.

The Imperative for Reproductive Justice

By Jane Marcus-Delgardo

After the overturning of Roe vs. Wade, an Ohio law prevents a girl from having an abortion. She eventually crosses into Indiana and medically terminates the pregnancy. It is determined that she has been pregnant for approximately six weeks and three days—a time at which many people don't even realize that their period is late. *She is ten years old.*

Abortion is one of the most prominent and controversial political, social, and cultural issues in the world. A quintessentially private medical procedure is now a topic for very public debates, thrusting questions of bodily autonomy and fundamental human justice into a harsh and unforgiving public sphere. The ten-year-old Ohio girl, the Honduran domestic worker, the Northern Irelanders forced to travel to England, and the Polish woman with a life-threatening pregnancy all share two traits in common. First, those affected are disproportionately from low-income, disempowered, and/or marginalized sectors of society. Second, their reproductive health depends on decisions subject to misogynistic, conservative (often religious), and opportunistic pressures from politicians, government officials, and weighty social stakeholders. Access to power and breaking the stigmatized silence of abortion are critical to making change.

Fortunately, recent setbacks in reproductive rights have catalyzed unprecedented grassroots mobilization. Poland's near-total abortion ban and the U.S. Supreme Court ruling ending the federal right to abortion are two examples of such draconian actions that have provoked widespread responses—and those countries' abortion justice activists join with millions worldwide to demand change. In recent decades, activism has emerged with three important and interconnected qualities that bode well for future success: technology, transnationalism, and intersectional solidarity.

Technology sheds light on the darkest corners of gender-based violence. Historically hidden abuses resulting in pregnancies, such as rape and incest, are increasingly exposed, as are back-alley abortions and "remedies" that can be harmful or fatal. People are outraged by cases such as those involving children, differently-abled individuals, and others—and their outrage turns to action. No one can claim ignorance of such violations. And, importantly, these revelations infuriate and spark participation in young adults, resulting in new

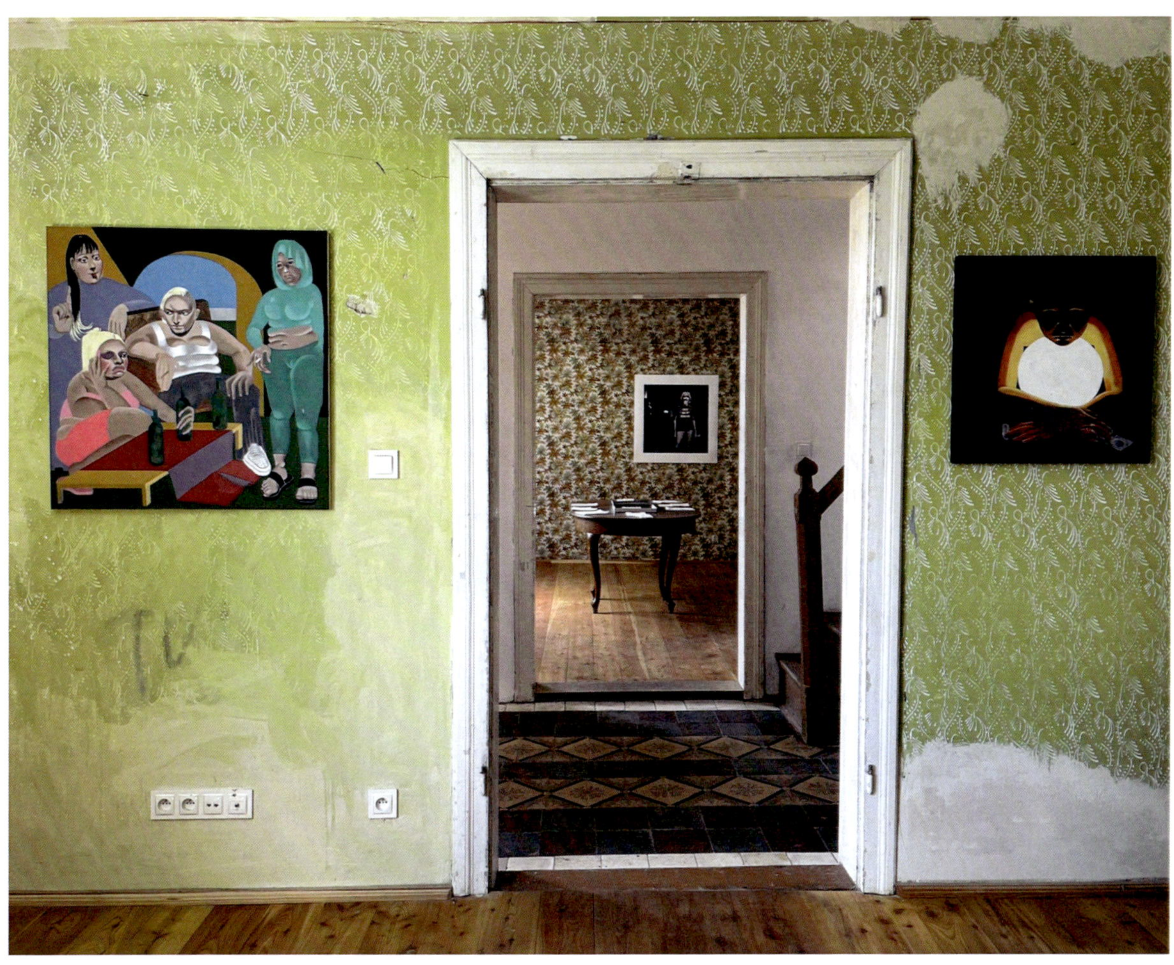

Installation shot of *Girls + Eggs* at CU AT SADKA, Krakow, Poland, 2022.

generations of motivated, energized, and creative activists.

Technology facilitates transnationalism and influences political culture. One of the most formidable efforts has been Latin America's "green wave" (*ola verde* in Spanish), a campaign in which activists began wearing green scarves to express support for abortion rights. Begun in Argentina, the scarves drew inspiration from the Mothers of the Plaza de Mayo, who wore white kerchiefs to demand justice for their children kidnapped by the military regime. The green wave spread from hundreds of thousands protesting in Argentina—an action that eventually aided in legalizing abortion—to protestors wearing green scarves throughout this hemisphere and in Europe. Prior to the 2023 election, thousands of Poles wore them in massive reproductive rights protests; the scarves have become a globally recognized symbol of the fight for abortion justice. And the Polish activists' efforts paid off, with voters rejecting a long-standing right-wing regime in favor of a more progressive coalition.

At the same time, transnational solidarity reaches far beyond the scarves' symbolic impact. Organizing for abortion justice permeates worldwide settings from art and creative expression to international courts and multinational organizations. The struggle is taking place in the classroom, in galleries, on the streets, in ballot boxes, and in courtrooms; it is massive, interconnected, and unstoppable.

Abortion justice advocacy is essentially intersectional—it cannot be separated from other feminist and gender-based struggles, or those involving workers, victims of racial and ethnic violence or people facing discrimination and prejudices. All of us must collectively channel our rage at the rise of right-wing nationalism, religious intolerance, sexism and misogyny, the militarization of our streets, mass incarceration, and other plagues. Defending the autonomy of our sexual and reproductive selves is where we can and must begin.

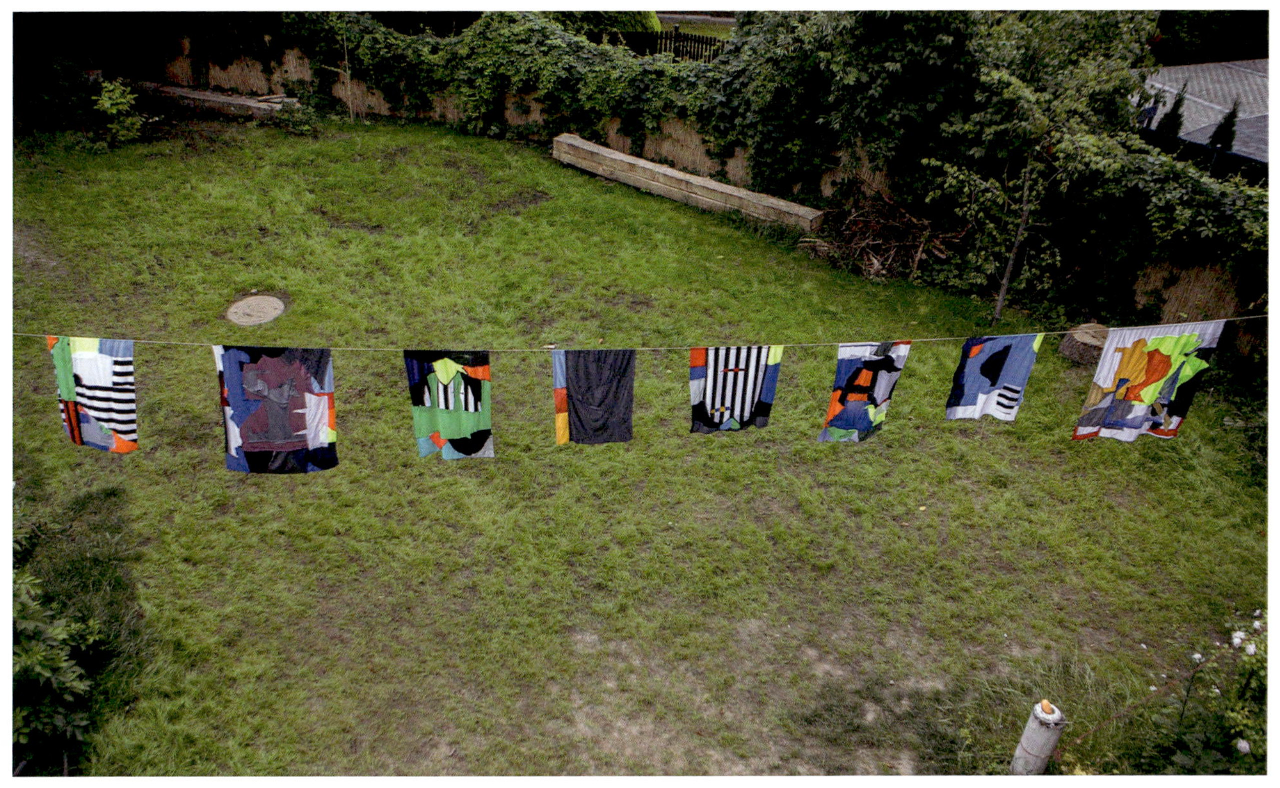

Michael Biber *Flags on a Line*, 2020, up cycled jersey off cuts, hot glue, polymer, sizes variable, shown at CU AT SADKA, 2022.

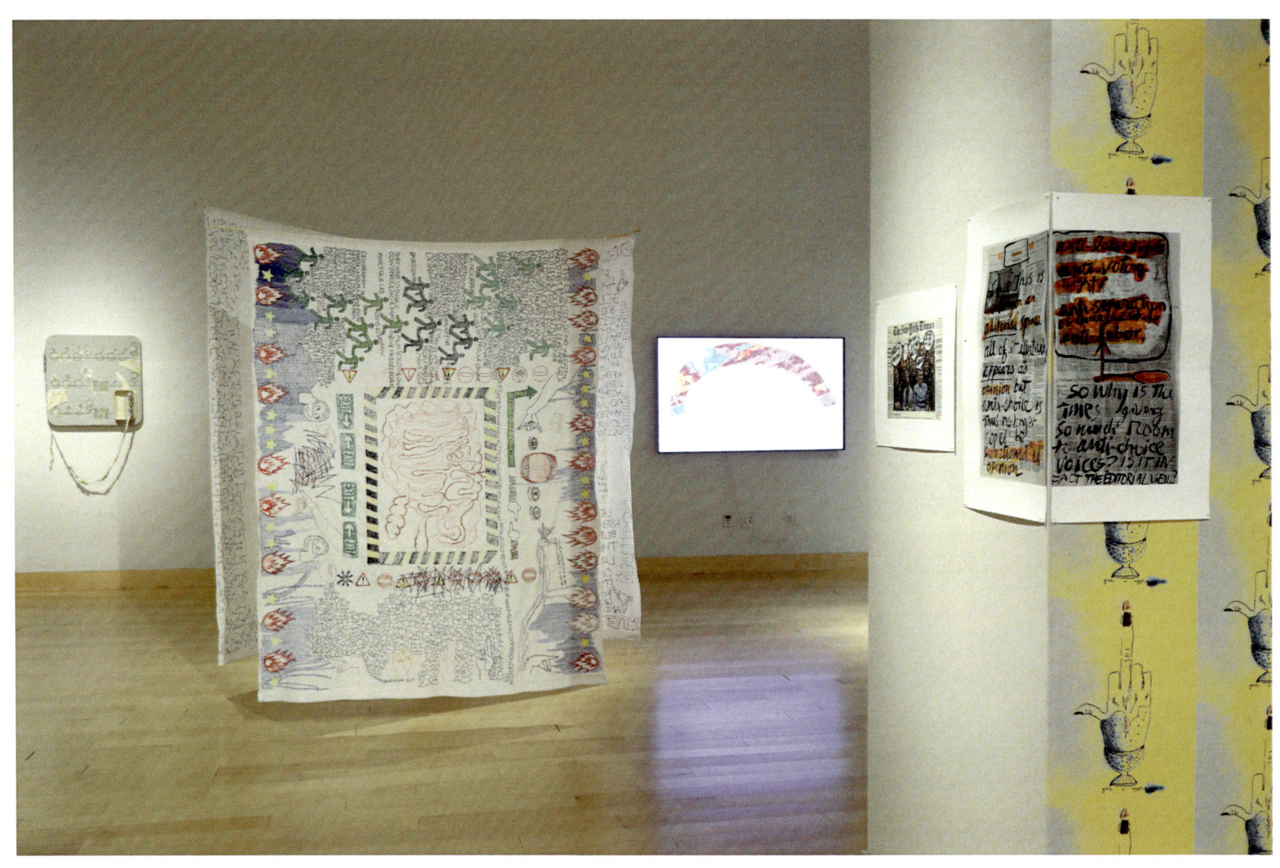

Installation shot of *Girls + Eggs* at Duke Hall Gallery of Fine Art, 2024.

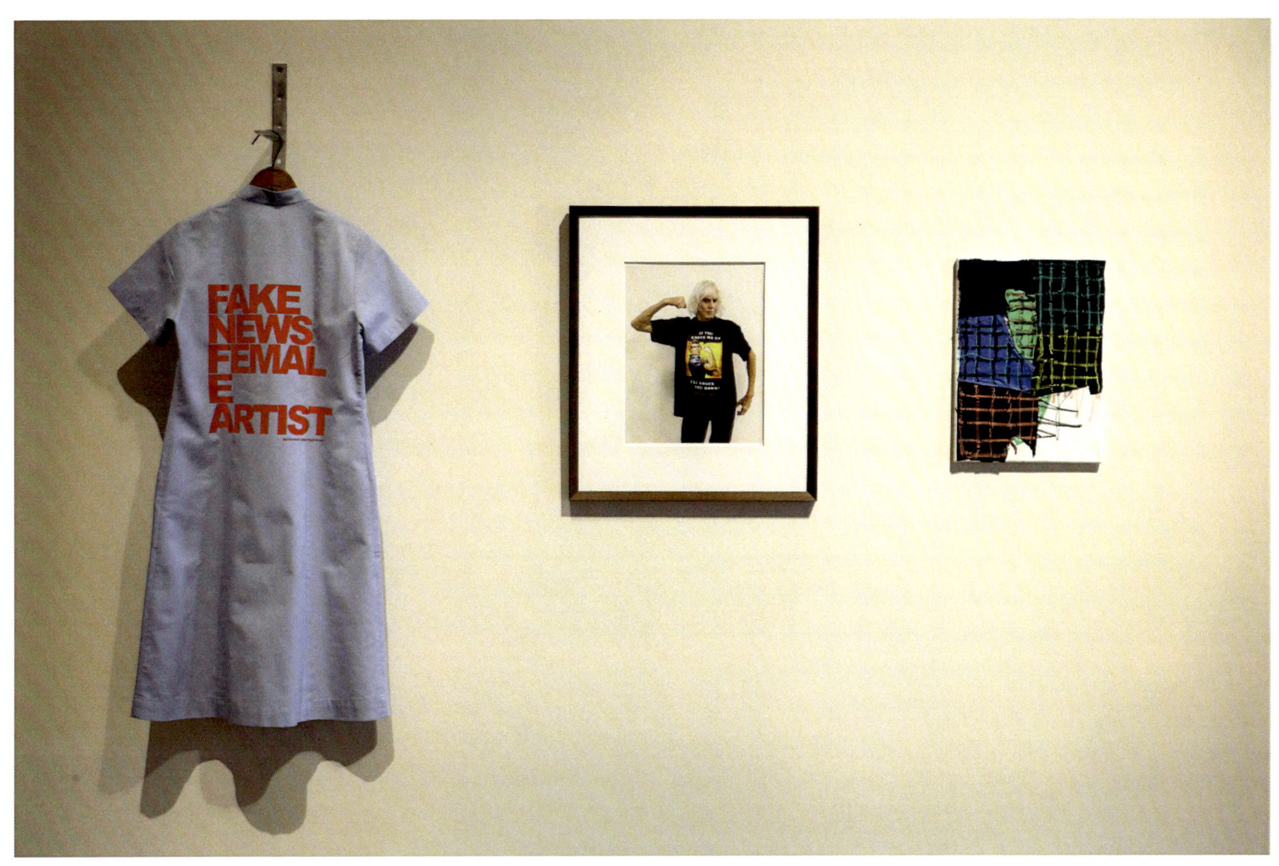

Installation shot of *Girls + Eggs* at Duke Hall Gallery of Fine Art, 2024.

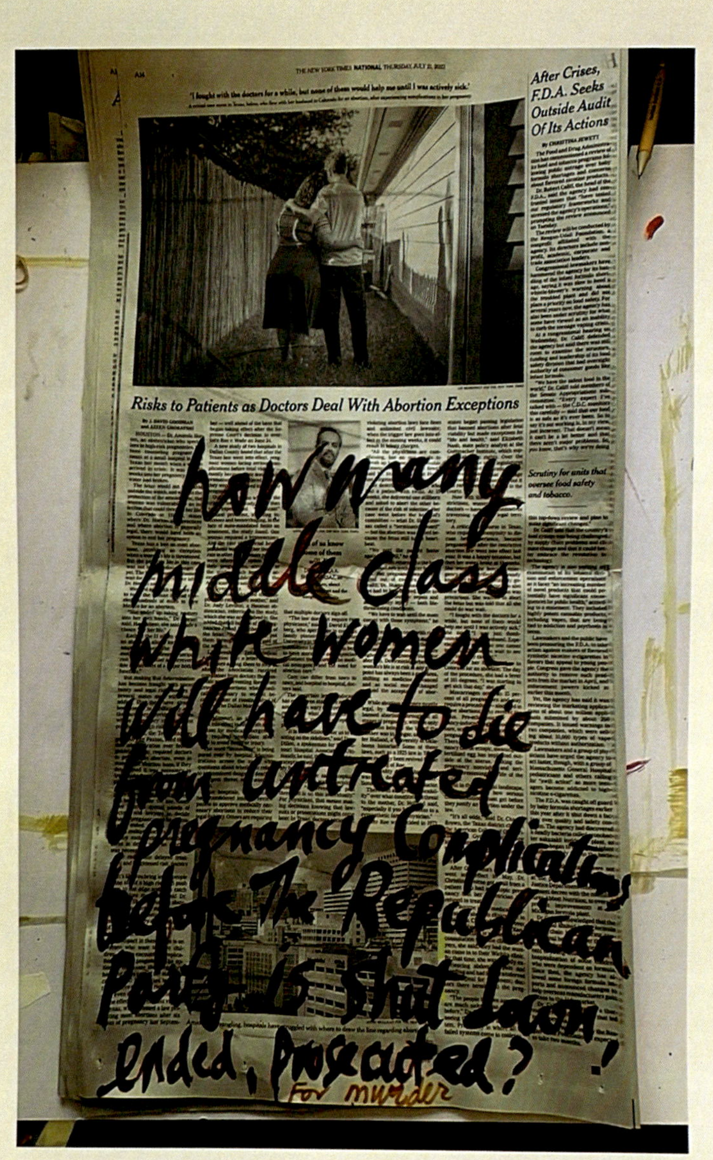

Mira Schor "How Many Middle-Class White Women" from *New York Time* Intervention, 2019-23, facsimile print, ink on New York Times, 21 x 29 inches.

It's a Lot

By Alyson Bardsley

They have already shared a lot. In the first five weeks of an evening Introduction to Women's Gender and Sexuality Studies class, students have told intimate stories of violent parents, creepy church elders, peers who mocked their sexuality, partners who policed their gender. During a break, one survivor is in tears in the hallway, two others, flanking her, murmur: "We made it out; we're here, we're here."

We call it "theorizing lived experience," but they are practicing it. They are witnessing each other's shit and calling things by their name.

Tonight's topic is Reproductive Justice. We use SisterSong's framework to think differently about reproductive rights. We talk about the right to be fertile, without a white supremacist state tying your BIPOC tubes as you recover from delivery; the right to give birth safely, and not succumb to the lethal neglect that takes the lives of especially Black laboring people and their babies in the US; the right to parent, and have your child not be poisoned by the environment or maimed by state agents. Reproductive Justice shows the gross inadequacy of the binary of Pro Choice and Anti Abortion, revealing it as a point located in a mare's nest of tangled forces, beliefs, and desires.

And yet. The choice in "Pro Choice" was once mine, and I made it, when I was as young as so many of these women. So, for once I tell my students, this group is the first. One woman huffs a laugh at a detail. "What?" I ask. "It's just. It's a lot," she explains, in sympathy. A couple more stories come: "I'm Pro Life," a woman says, describing leaving the clinic "everyone" had urged her to use, since she had no job and no man, "but that's just me, that's just me." "You keep saying you're Pro Life," another tells her, "but also keep saying you wouldn't tell anyone else what to do. That means you're Pro Choice, you realize that?" I worry aloud that my years (and years, and years) of silence have somehow helped lead the country to this pass, where my choice now isn't open to other women. Another woman agrees: she had an abortion in her birthplace, a country that has since made it completely illegal, and she feels guilty, not about her choice, but about its foreclosure to others.

So, we finish by listing what we'd need to do to solve the problem of unwanted pregnancies. Their list includes, stop shaming single mothers; equal pay; ending rape culture; free contraception; adequate sexual education; access to health care, childcare, decent schools. One woman says, "make the world a place you'd actually want to bring a child into."

I scrub their list off the white board once they're gone

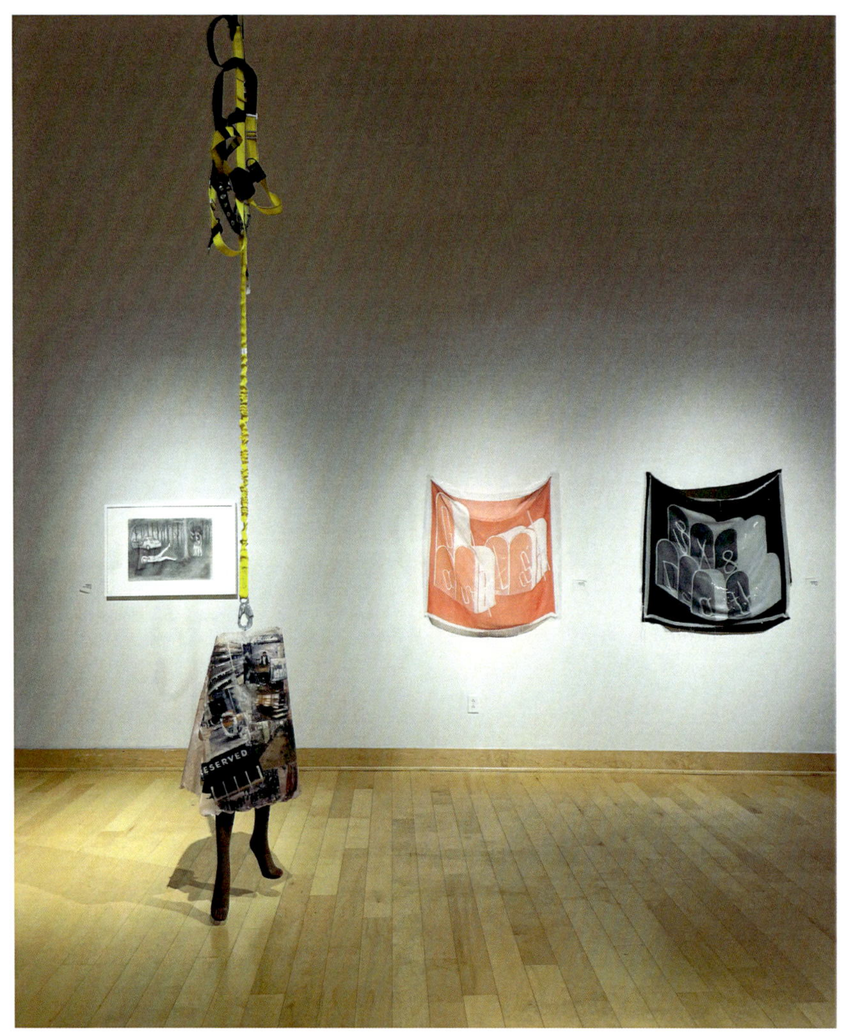

Installation shot of *Girls + Eggs* at Duke Hall Gallery of Fine Art, 2024.

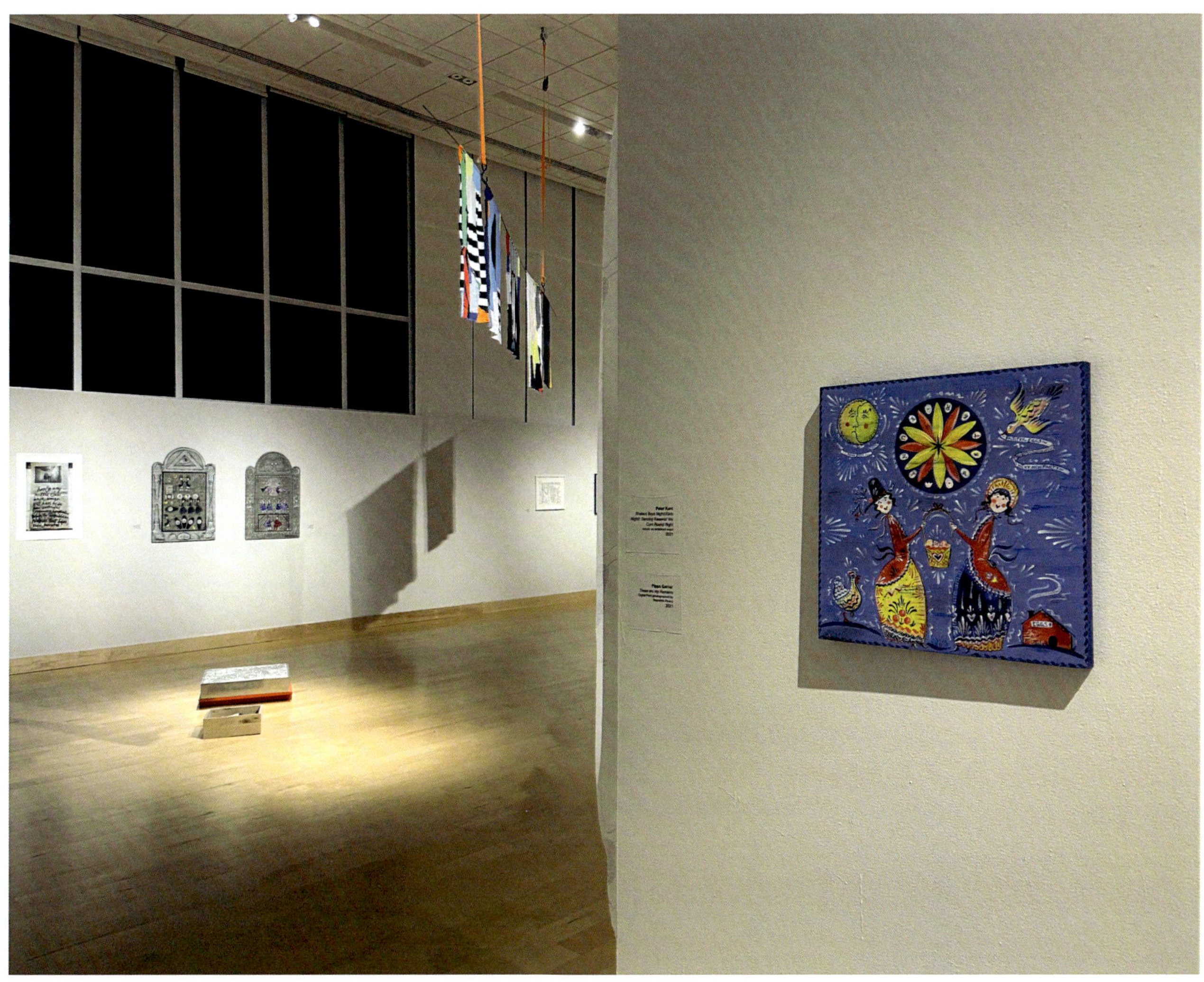

Installation shot of *Girls + Eggs* at Duke Hall Gallery of Fine Art, 2024
FOREGROUND Peter Kunt, *Ea(s)ter Eggs—Hexy Hen Party Hex*, 2022, acrylic on board

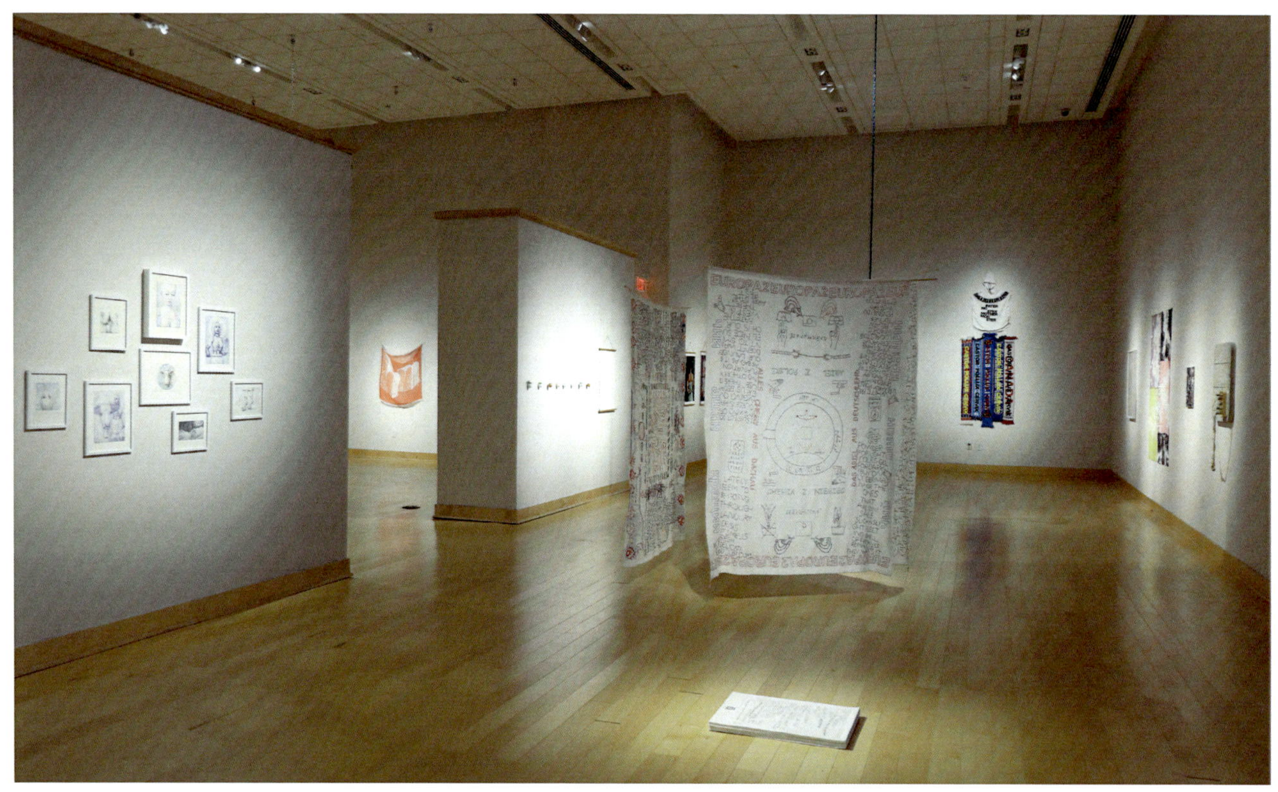

Installation shot of *Girls + Eggs* at Duke Hall Gallery of Fine Art, 2024.

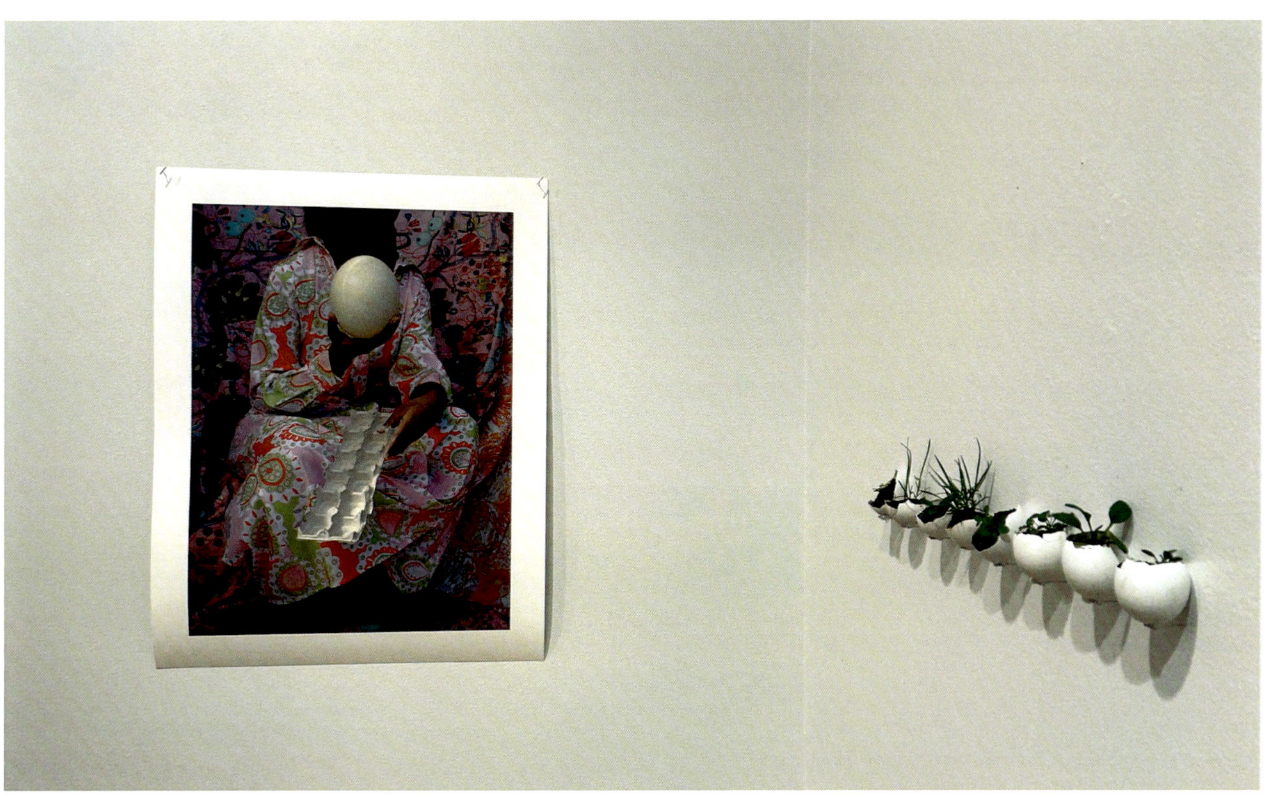

Beatrix Reinhardt *Untitled [Eggs + J]*, 2022, archival pigment print with Reinhardt *Untitled (Temporary Sculptures)* 2022/4, egg shelves and found weeds.

Afterword: Roe Means Eggs

Beth Hinderliter

In Beatrix Reinhardt's photograph *Untitled [Eggs + J]* (2022), a woman holds an ostrich egg, which is too large to fit into the chicken egg carton that she holds in her other hand. Her pink clothes and the pink fabric draped in the background channel as well as satirize the "pink think" that historically solely equates femininity with delicacy, blushing cheeks, and a supposedly unbreakable association with sexuality and sexual reproduction. The outsized ostrich egg contributes to this feeling of fecundity by relating a female human to this giant bird. In an anatomy book published in 1829, Scottish anatomist John Barclay compares a female human skeleton with that of an ostrich. The skeleton's small skull was likened to a bird brain and her large bowl-shaped pelvis was said to be thus shaped to ensure fecundity. Without the natural reason supposedly associated with men's larger brains, women were anatomically as well as morally predetermined to play one social role: producing babies. The ostrich egg has many other associations as well, from the symbol of fertility and purity poised on top of the spire of Malian mosques, to a general sign of largesse. Within the exhibition *Girls + Eggs* and in the context of the post-Roe vs. Wade (2022) environment in the United States, Reinhardt's work critiques the status of females being once more reduced to their procreative abilities—the equivalent of an ostrich.

Creating local, national, and international bonds of solidarity, the exhibition *Girls + Eggs* screams at the increasing irrelevance of human rights in our post-Roe vs. Wade era. We are not human. We are ostriches. With humor, anger, and sass, the artists in the exhibition challenge restrictive definitions of gender and sexuality, refute the relegation of childrearing to the hidden domestic sphere, ask who has the economic capacity to take care of their children, and demand the right to healthcare and accurate information on issues such as abortion.

If you crack an ostrich egg, is a human born?

Right-wing fanatics in the United States have resurrected pre-1960s debates over legal access to abortion and acceptable healthcare, seeking to foreclose the demands for autonomy, individual choice, as well as the broader social demands for equity launched by the reproductive justice movement of the 1990s. In other countries around the world, new restrictions or new total bans on abortion procedures jeopardize the global access of women to life-enabling and life-saving healthcare. States of uncertainty, emergency, and panic over which bodies can occupy which spaces openly,

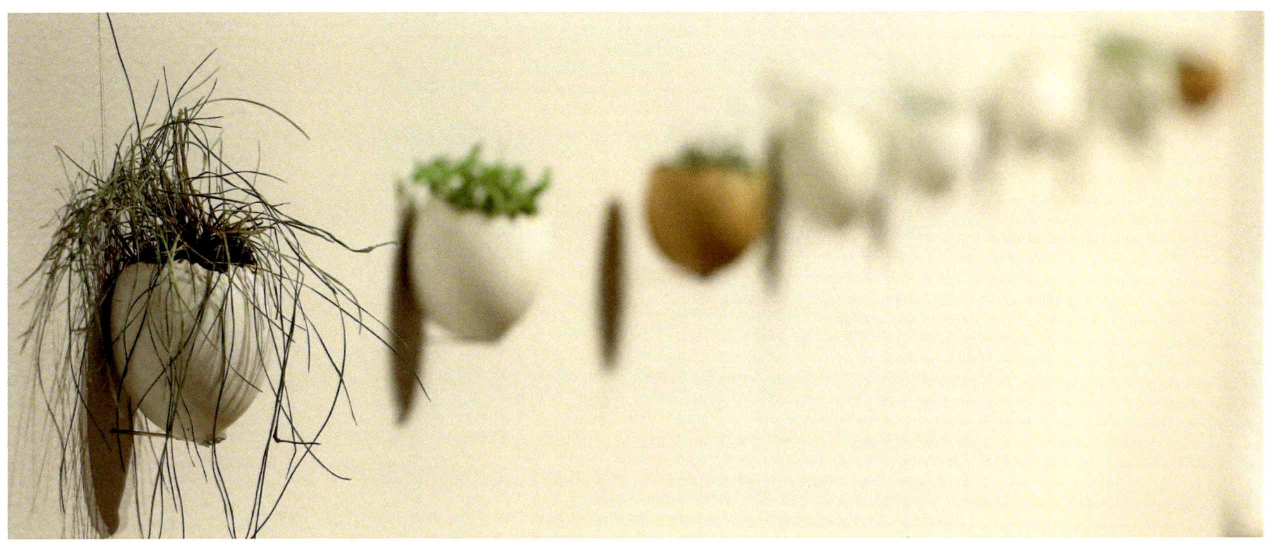

Beatrix Reinhardt *Untitled (Temporary Sculptures)* 2022/4, egg shelves and found weeds.

are used to justify increased state intervention. In 2020, Poland's then right wing government imposed a near to total ban on abortion. Since then, the Dobbs ruling in 2022 in the US overturned the protections on abortion provided by the Roe vs. Wade decision of 1973. Twenty-one states across the US have imposed new restrictions or bans on abortion. The conversations generated in *Girls + Eggs* between different states in the US as well as across international boundaries fortify these receding boundaries between individual and democratic self-determination and this increasing authoritarian impulse. Virginia remains the only Southern state whose laws and restrictions around abortion have remained unchanged since 2022. As I write this, many women travel to Virginia from other Southern states to receive healthcare here and recent statistics reveal that 70-75% of Virginians want to maintain the status quo of access to abortion or have fewer restrictions.

The 1973 decision of Roe vs Wade centered on the right to privacy protected by the Fourteenth Amendment, which prohibits states from "depriv[ing] any person of liberty without due process of law." Freedom or autonomy of individual choice was key to the advocacy work of many national groups such as the National Organization for Women (NOW). The well-known motif of 1970s mainstream feminism, "the personal is political," focused largely on individual freedoms while recognizing the social, cultural, and legal protections required to improve the status of womens' lives. In the 1990s, reproductive justice advocates in the US, such as the organization, SisterSong, shifted the focus of abortion from women's rights to "choose" to broader questions of reproductive justice and the interplay of individual and collective rights. Based on an inclusive human right focus, the reproductive justice movement asserts that we all have the right to control our bodies and to decide how our families are structured. Activists and scholars like Loretta Ross of SisterSong have asserted that our individual rights and legal access to safe and effective healthcare, including abortions, are only part of the larger socio-economic structure that determines women's ability to control their own reproductive destinies. To have sovereignty over your reproductive destiny entails working to remove all the limiting factors such as poverty, lack of transportation, racial barriers, and many more socio-cultural barriers, not just for the right to have a child or not, but also as Ross has said, the right to parent the children you may already have.

We might ask, *what does bodily autonomy look like in the post-Roe era*?

Is autonomy a space? Is it a feeling? A relationship? A diagram of power? Is it the network of women's clinics that facilitate a space of care but which currently face being shuttered across the US? Is it the right to choose your name and where it appears in court documents, the news, or on signs? Jane Roe chose anonymity when she fought her battle in court to secure an abortion. Many women in the US who now find themselves engulfed in this same fight are choosing to give their real names. What does privacy mean in our era of digital surveillance capitalism and how can we ensure meaningful privacy when we need it? What autonomy, however temporary, can be generated in the conversations around this exhibition? The lines of sight throughout the gallery space offered to the viewers have been carefully crafted by curator Siona Wilson to break down rigid associations of gender and sexual stereotypes and definitions. There are moments of joy and resistance as well as anger and fatigue at our retrograde autonomy.

What we learn is that Roe means eggs.

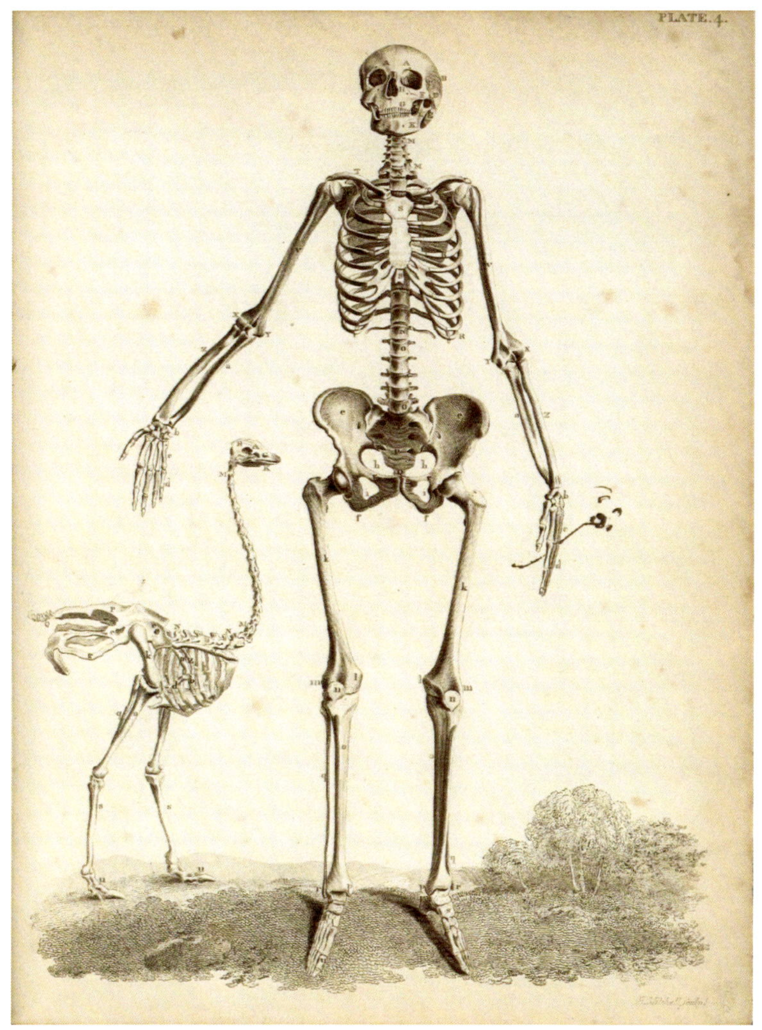

John Barclay, *The Anatomy of the Bones of the Human Body*; Represented in a Series of Engravings, Copied from the Elegent [sic] tables of Sue and Albinus. Edward Mitchell, engraver, Maclachlan and Steward: 1829. Public domain image.

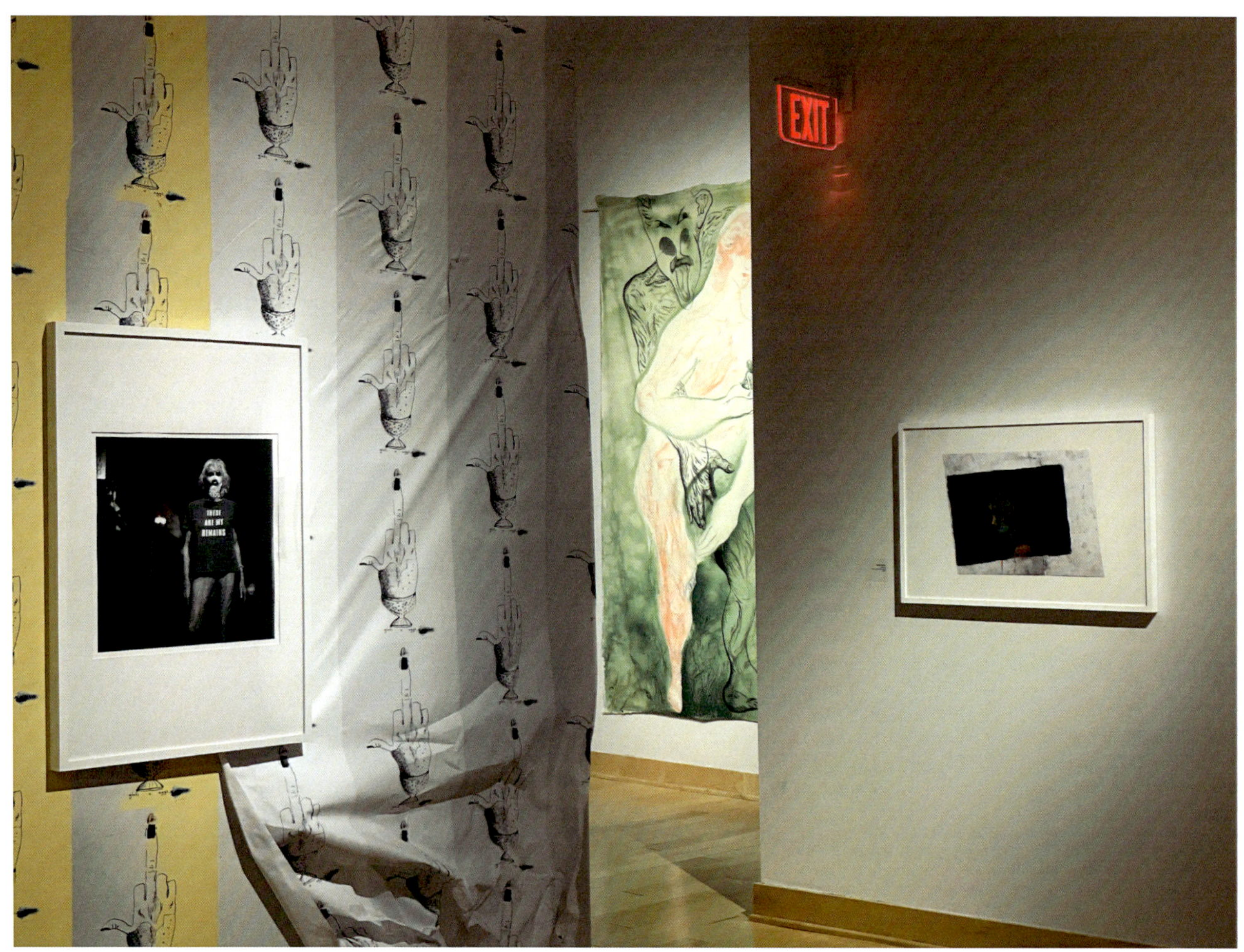

Installation shot of *Girls + Eggs* at Duke Hall Gallery of Fine Art, 2024.

Author Biographies

Dr. Alyson Bardsley is an Associate Professor in the English Department and the Program in Women's, Gender, and Sexuality Studies at The College of Staten Island, The City University of New York (CUNY). Her current research and teaching interests include feminist science studies and disabilities in literature and culture. She received her PhD in English from the University of California at Berkeley.

Dr. Beth Hinderliter is the Director of the Duke Hall Gallery of Fine Art and Associate Professor of Art History at James Madison University, Virginia. As a curator she works inclusively to create contemporary art exhibitions engaged in the care of new possible worlds and social relations. Previous exhibitions include *Visible to the User, Colonial Wounds/Postcolonial Repair, Skeena Reece, Honey and Sweetgrass,* and *Exuberance: Dialogues in African American Abstract Painting.* She is the co-editor of *More than Our Pain: Affect and Emotion in the Era of Black Lives Matter* (SUNY Press, 2021) as well as *Communities of Sense: Rethinking Aesthetics and Politics* (Duke University Press, 2008). Her essays appear in *NKA, Journal of Postcolonial Writing, TDR, African and Black Diaspora,* and *October.*

Dr. Jane Marcus-Delgado is a Professor of political science at The College of Staten Island (CUNY) who specializes in Latin American studies. Jane is the acting Executive Officer of the Latin American, Iberian and Latino Cultures doctoral program at the CUNY Graduate Center. Her book, *The Politics of Abortion in Latin America*: *Public Debates Over Private Lives,* was published by Lynne Rienner in 2020.

Dr. Siona Wilson is Associate Professor of Art History at the College of Staten Island (CUNY) and the Director of the Art Gallery. She is also on the doctoral faculty at the Graduate Center (CUNY). Her research interests are grounded in issues of sexual difference, race, and sexuality at the intersection of art and politics in the twentieth century. Author of *Art Labor, Sex Politics: Feminist Effects in 1970s British Art and Performance* (Minnesota, 2014), she has published on photography, experimental film, video, sound, and performance art, in edited collections and journals, including *Art History, October, Oxford Art Journal* and *Third Text*. Her recent curatorial projects include *I can't breathe*, at the Gallery of the College of Staten Island, featuring works in video and photography by Nona Faustine, Patricia Silva, Emma Wolukau-Wanambwa and Kara Walker with a timeline of images documenting the activist group, Staten Islanders Against Racism and Police Brutality (SIARPB). She also co-curated *Sexing Sound: Aural Archives and Feminist Scores* (with Valerie Tevere and Catherine Karl) at the James Gallery, New York. Professor Wilson's new research relates to documentary, gender, and state violence in a diverse range of geographic sites, including Algeria, Britain, "Kurdistan," Iraq and Vietnam, focusing on episodes from the 1930s to the present.

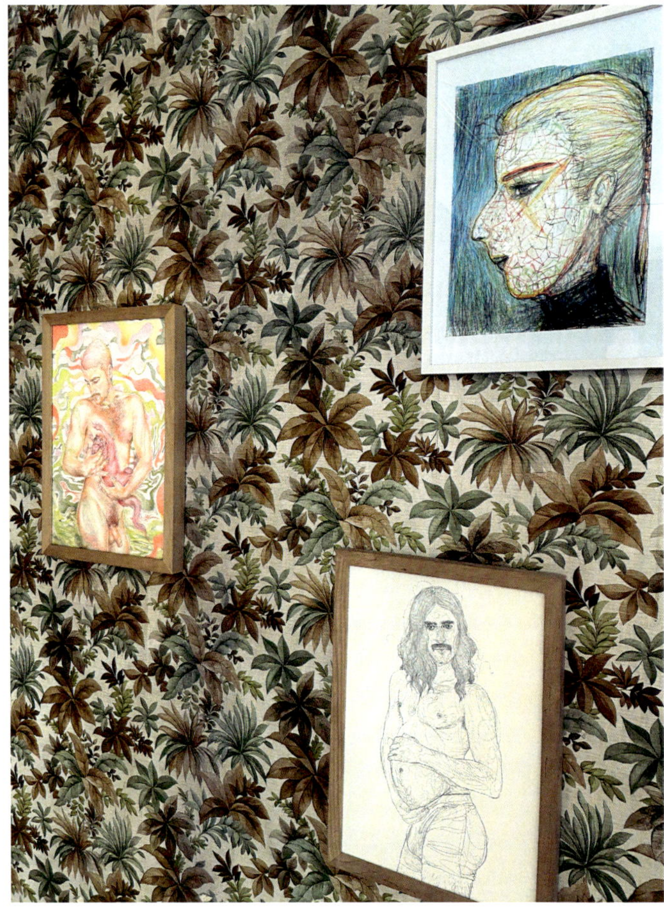

TOP RIGHT	Oskar Korsar *Untitled*, 2021, crayon on paper
BOTTOM RIGHT	Bartek Arobal Kociemba, *Pregnant Self Portrait*, 2016, pencil on paper
LEFT	Bartek Arobal Kociemba, *Breastfeeding*, 2022, color pencil on paper

Artist Biographies

Michael Biber lives and works in Krakow and Berlin.
Born 1978
Graduation School 1995
Education for painting 1995-1998
Education for classical sculpture 1999-2003
Practica for scenery at Residenztheater, Munich. 2003
Studied painting at Academy of Fine Arts, Akademie der Bildenden Künste, Munich, with
Prof. Markus Oehlen. 2003/04
Prof. Sean Scully. 2004/06
Prof. Günther Förg 2006/09
Master's student with Prof. Günther Förg 2008
2009 Diploma
2009 Prize for Debutants of Akademie der Bildenenden Künste, Munich
2012 Art Prize of the state of Bavaria
2015 became Father of my son Mikolaj
2021 co-founded C U at Sadka
2022 represented by UFO Gallery, Krakow

Martyna Borowiecka was born in 1989 in Kielce, Poland. In 2013 she graduated with distinction from the Academy of Fine Arts in Cracow, studying Painting and Fashion Design. In 2019 she received her PhD. Borowiecka has participated in several individual and group exhibitions and has won many competitions such as The National Painting Competition, VII Triennial with Still Life organized by BWA in Sieradz, as well as the Grand Prix of the Minister of Culture and National Heritage, PL (2015). She lives and works between Cracow and Wieliczka, Poland.

Magda Buczek is a Warsaw and Copenhagen-based multidisciplinary artist and the founder of SURPLUS and co-founder of VI LEVER PÅ POLSK, an artist-run space in Copenhagen. Buczek tells multilayered stories from the perspective of a mother, feminist, and Eastern European. The main tools of her practice are text, fashion, and waste. She received two awards from the Statens Kunstfond Denmark in 2022, a special work grant in 2020, and an invitation for art residency at Academia di Danimarca in Rome in 2022. Recent exhibitions include Super Dakota in Brussels (2022), the RA show at Royal Academy of Arts in London (2021), Art Hub Copenhagen (2020), and Biennale Warszawa (2019).

Kat Chamberlin's works have been exhibited across the U.S. and internationally and featured in exhibitions at the Museum of Contemporary Art in Chicago, the Chicago Cultural Center, Barbara and Steven Grossman Gallery in Boston, and BRIC in New York City. Kat completed her MFA at the School of the Art Institute of Chicago and is the recipient of a Jacob K. Javits Fellowship, the Toby Devan Lewis Award, and the William Dole Award. As a Swedish-Armenian, Kat was born in the Netherlands and raised in Ankara, Turkey; she currently works and lives in Brooklyn. "I'm a drawer in a cabinet full of emotional responses, abstract thoughts, and conceptual objects. My drawing and sculptural works are an analog response to a digital scroll of consciousness."

Moyra Davey is a New York-based artist whose work comprises the fields of photography, film, and writing. She is the author of *Index Cards, Burn the Diaries, The Problem of Reading*, and is the editor of *Mother Reader: Essential Writings on Motherhood. The Shabbiness of Beauty*, a book of photographs by Peter Hujar and Davey, with a text by Eileen Myles, was published by Mack Books, London in 2021. Davey's work is held in major public collections, including the Museum of Modern Art and the Metropolitan Museum of Art in New York, and Tate Modern in London. She is a 2020 recipient of the John S. Guggenheim Memorial Foundation Fellowship.

Piotr Dluzniewski was born 1952 in Lodz, Poland. In 1958 he moved to Germany. For many years P. Dluzniewski has lived mostly in Cologne where he has a studio, but he also makes work while travelling. Solo exhibitions include: 1993 Galerie Otto Schweins, Köln; 1995 Air de Paris, Paris; 1997 Second Sunday, Köln; 2001 Gitti Nourbakhsch Galerie Berlin; 2005 Comme ci Comme ca II,(Karin Barth), Köln; 2008 "The neverending story of beautiful shoes, surprising turns of fate and the cows of Berner Oberland," 1m3, Lausanne; 2009 "Better Homes and Gardens with Modern Art and Cows," Laurent Godin, Paris; 2011 "Die Alm," Galerie Konzett, Wien; 2019 "Paturages," Galerie Laurent Godin, Paris.

Monika Drożyńska is a visual artist-embroiderer-activist and PhD researcher at Academy of Fine Arts Cracow, Poland. A pioneer of embroidery techniques in contemporary art and textiles in public space. She is interested in language, which she explores using hand embroidery on fabric. She has collaborated with the Zachęta National Gallery of Art, the Center for Contemporary Art Ujazdowski Castle, the Contemporary Museum in Wroclaw, Mumok in Vienna, the Ludwig Museum in Budapest, Bozar in Brussels, Sotheby's, and Tel Aviv, Manifesta 14 Prishtina, 2022. Her work has been collected by Bunkier Sztuki, National Museum in Krakow, Mocak Museum of Contemporary Art in Cracow, National Museum in Kiev, and Lentos in Austria.

Pippa Garner was born in 1942 in the Chicago suburb of Evanston, Illinois, the U.S.-American artist, and author formerly known as Philip Garner, is pushing back against systems of consumerism, marketing, and waste, and has created a dense body of work including drawing, performance, sculpture, video, and installation over her five-decade-long career. Her uncompromising approach to life and practice has allowed her to interact with the worlds of illustration, editorial, television, and art without ever quite becoming beholden to them.

After serving in Vietnam as a combat artist, Garner began her practice in the 1960s when she was studying as a member of the highly regarded Transportation Design Department at ArtCenter, California with plans to become a car stylist. Garner's circle during the 1970s and 1980s included West Coast artists Ed Ruscha, Chris Burden, and the radical art and design collective Ant Farm. Garner (then identifying and known as Phil) gained attention for her performance, design, and video work at galleries and museums, such as the Museum of Contemporary Art, Los Angeles, and the Whitney Museum of American Art, New York, and appearances on the Tonight Show Starring Johnny Carson, and other talk shows showcasing her satirical consumer product "inventions." Her art has appeared in *Car & Driver*, *Rolling Stone*, *Arts & Architecture*, and *Vogue*, among other publications.

Pippa Garner has lived and worked primarily in California for more than fifty years and is currently based in Long Beach. Recent solo exhibitions include *Act Like You Know Me*, Kunstverein, Munich (2022), Joan, Los Angeles (2022); STARS, Los Angeles (2021); Jeffrey Stark, New York (2021); O-Town House, Los Angeles (2019); Redling Fine Art, Los Angeles (2017, 2018); and Parker Gallery, Los Angeles (2015). Garner's work has been reviewed in *Artforum*, *Los Angeles Times*, *Hyperallergic*, *Interview*, *L'Officiel Art*, *Spike*, and *X-tra*.

Jakub Hošek is a non-binary painter, curator, DJ, cultural activist, and co-founder of the A. M. 180 collective, which connects art & music and organizes concerts and the alternative music festival *Creepy Teepee*. Hošek is also co-head of the painting studio (PAINT III) at the Academy of Fine Arts in Prague. "As sharp the lines can get, as honest the statement speaks, as happy, as sad, as awkward, as fragile always get, their style is always changing, but never turns a different direction, so the thorns will jab you with heart-breaking realness forever."

Maria Kniaginin-Ciszewska was born in 1998 in Warsaw. In 2021 she graduated in photography from the Royal Academy of Fine Arts in The Hague. Her interests revolve around stereotypes and their presentation in culture. As an independent visual artist, she works between reality and fantasy, penetrating social and cultural norms. By creating representations of the female form, she examines the boundaries of taboos and icons. She explores the artifacts of Polishness or, more broadly, Slavicness, combining them with the concepts of the body and interpersonal relations.

Bartek Arobal Kociemba (born 1984) is a visual artist, draftsman, and illustrator. Since 2006, he has produced illustrations for most Polish magazines. He has collaborated with the Teatr Dramatyczny and the Grand Theater, the National Opera. Creator of many theater and film posters. Author of many book illustrations and covers and music albums among others by Monika Brodka, Fisz and Emade, and Stefan Weglowski. His recent solo projects include *What's Hidden* 2019, presented at the Silesian Museum in Katowice and *Whole-burnt Flowers* 2021, presented at the Municipal Gallery Arsenal in Poznan *Flowers burning* 2022, presented at the Overtrappen Gallery in Copenhagen *Queer meditation* 2019, an ongoing performative/educational project. His works were presented among others in Biała Gallery in Lublin, Leto Gallery in Warsaw, the Museum of Modern Art in Warsaw, the Poster Museum in Wilanów, at the Trafostacja in Szczecin, and at exhibitions and art fairs in Berlin, Copenhagen, London, Rome, and New York. In 2020, together with Magda Buczek, he started an artist-run space and gallery VI LEVER PÅ POLSK located in Copenhagen, Denmark. Since 2021 he has been represented by Warsaw based Szydłowski Gallery.

Oskar Korsár is a Swedish artist based in Berlin (b. 1977, Umeä, Sweden). He studied Graphic Design and Illustration at Konstfack University of Arts, Crafts and Design in Stockholm. Solo exhibitions include *I Like Feminism and Feminism Likes me* at the Art Gallery of the College of Staten Island, New York (2022), a mid-career retrospective, Fullersta Gård, Stockholm, Sverige (2017); *Unidentified Archaeological Findings*, Borås Konsthall, Borås, Jönköpings Konsthall, Prins Eugens Waldemarsudde, Stockholm (2016); *No Wind Can Blow Us Down*, Yossi Milo Gallery, New York, USA (2007). Recent group exhibition: *Machine Gun Etiquette*, Belmacz, London (2018); *Wrestling Performance*, Gagnef Festival, Sweden (2016); Konst i ån, Nortällje Konsthall, Norrtälje, Sweden (2016). His work is in the public collections of: Moderna Museet, Stockholm, Sweden; Statens Konstråd, Sweden; and Stockholm Stad, Sweden. He has held positions as a Senior Lecturer at Brunnsviks konstskola, Sweden and a visiting professor of integrated design, Hochschule für Künste Bremen, Staatliche Universität in Bremen, Germany.

Maja Krysiak was born in 1980 in Częstochowa, Poland, she lives and works in Krakow. She is a visual artist specializing in painting and drawing. Her work explores historical and personal issues and touches upon themes of spirituality, femininity, and dreams. In 2005, she graduated with honors from the Painting Department at the Academy of Fine Arts in Krakow. She obtained her Ph.D with honors at the Academy of Fine Arts in Krakow in 2023. She has had six solo exhibitions and has participated in many group exhibitions and workshops. Currently she teaches drawing at the Academy of Fine Arts in Krakow. Dreams play a very important role in the artist's work, as she has been carefully documenting them for years and used them as the primary inspiration for her painterly compositions. Dreams allow her to delve into the subconscious, search for archetypes, and construct vivid metaphors. Reality and dream are seamlessly intertwined in her work. She finds their afterimages in everyday activities, like imprints on a pillow. For years, Krysiak has built her artistic imagination and metaphorical language around the figure of a travelling circus full of human and animal oddities, including dwarves, giants, clowns, acrobats and wild, exotic creatures. She sees them as Foucauldian heterotopias, "other" places that operate according to their own rules. The vibrant colors and dynamism of the circus become a metaphor for her struggles with the subconscious and the unconscious.

Peter Kunt (as Sean F. Edgecomb) is Associate Professor of Theatre at Fairfield University. His work focuses on queer theory, inclusive histories and the hybrid relationship between scholarship and performance (broadly defined). His books include *Charles Ludlam Lives!: Charles Busch, Bradford Louryk, Taylor Mac and the Queer Legacy of the Ridiculous Theatre Company* (2017) and *The Taylor Mac Book:*

Ritual, Realness and Radical Performance (2023). His current book project, A *Queer Bestiary*, examines LGBTQIA+ performance artists who engage animal symbolism and/or ritual anthropomorphism in their work, reconsidering queer cultural migration through the lens of the folkloric. He has published scholarly articles in journals as well as many book chapters in edited collections. He has painted queer folk art as his sobriquet "Peter Kunt" since 2020. Peter Kunt was created as a performative extension of his work as a queer artist and LGBTQIA+ theatre scholar. As Kunt, Edgecomb is committed to creating original work that resurrects queer voices of the past that have been silenced, forgotten, and erased. This work reframes naive, folkloric techniques (distinct brushwork) and compositions (often geometric or symmetrical) drawn from early settler colonists and immigrants to what would become the United States.

Madeline Kuzak (b. 1993, Detroit, MI) is an artist who lives and works in Brooklyn. She uses a variety of media to explore imagery sourced from fetish art, stock photos, film, or her psyche. She is mainly concerned with imagery that is banal, libidinal, and abject. She has presented her work nationally and internationally. Most recently she's staged solo exhibitions at Darkzone (New Jersey) and In Lieu (LA). She has also participated in group exhibitions at Shoot the Lobster (NYC), Baitball #2 (Italy), ASHES/ASHES (NYC) and Mickey Gallery (Chicago).

Danni O'Brien (she/they), b. 1992 in Virginia, is a queer, interdisciplinary artist working between Baltimore, Maryland and Central Kansas. O'Brien received their BFA in Sculpture from James Madison University in 2014. Her work has been exhibited with Asya Geisberg Gallery, Museum of Contemporary Art Arlington, Belger Arts Center, and the Virginia Museum of Contemporary Art. She has been awarded residencies with PLOP (London, UK), Proyecto Ace (Buenos Aires, Argentina), Baltimore Clayworks, and Art Farm, among others. In 2023 they were a resident artist at Stove Works, Elizabeth Murray Artist Residency, and Wassaic Project. Her 2022 solo exhibition, Cross Sections, with Tephra ICA, was reviewed in the Washington Post. O'Brien had her debut solo exhibition, *Wa(r)ning Light* with Ortega y Gasset Projects in 2024.

Beatrix Reinhardt grew up in Jena, Germany. After the completion of her undergraduate studies in New German Literature at the Freie Universität Berlin she planned to study at the New School for Social Research in New York for one year. The one year became two and Reinhardt graduated with an M.A. in Media Studies. While at the New School, she started her studies in photography, which she continued at Illinois State University. Since the completion of a Master of Fine Arts degree, Reinhardt has been living, working, curating, and teaching in different parts of the world. She has been invited as artist-in-residence to universities and galleries in Finland, India, South Africa, Australia, China, Turkey, Vietnam, and the US, among others. In 2005 she was appointed at City University of New York/CUNY and lives and works most of the year in Queens, N.Y.

Mira Schor (b. 1950, New York, US) is a New York based artist and writer. Her work has been included in exhibitions at The Jewish Museum, New York, US; The Hammer Museum, Los Angeles, US; MoMA P.S.1, New York, US; Kunsthaus Graz, AT; and Kestner Gesellschaft, Hanover, DE. Schor is the recipient of many prestigious awards including the Guggenheim Fellowship in Painting, the Pollock-Krasner Grant, the College Art Association's Frank Jewett Mather Award in Art Criticism, the Creative Capital / Warhol Foundation Arts Writers Grant, and the 2019 Women's Caucus for Art Lifetime Achievement Award for her work as a feminist painter, art historian, and critic. She is the author of *A Decade of Negative Thinking: Essays on Art, Politics, and Daily Life* and *Wet: On Painting, Feminism, and Art Culture*, and of the blog "A Year of Positive Thinking." She was the co-founder and co-editor with fellow painter Susan Bee of the journal *M/E/A/N/I/N/G*. Schor's work is in the permanent collections of Carnegie Museum of Art, Pittsburgh, US; Minneapolis Institute of Art, Minneapolis, US; The Marieluise Hessel Collection of Contemporary

Art, Annandale-on- Hudson, US; Pennsylvania Academy of the Fine Arts, Philadelphia, US. She is an Associate Teaching Professor in Fine Arts at Parsons, The New School for Design. Schor is represented by Lyles & King, New York.

Agnieszka Szostek (b. 1982 in Cracow) is the co-founder of C U at Sadka. She is a Polish visual artist based in Berlin and Cracow. Her practice blends homemade printing techniques, a tender mix of artificial and natural elements, fading collages, and online aesthetics. Her materials are sophisticated, but still close to human touch. Recent exhibitions include *PPS: it's a progressive fantasy (...)* co-curated with Tristan Deschamps at C U AT SADKA in Cracow, PL 2021. Recent group exhibitions include *A Californian Plumber* @hei.fugitive Leibzig DE, 2020, *DIO E' C'* Ultrastudio Pescara, IT 2020, *Die Bestehende Realität (Prozess und Tanz)* video presentation at Gallery Bark Berlin DE 2020, *Home Invasion* 24/7 online on Arbyte On Screen, London 2019, *Come What May. Permanent Assumptions*, Zner Kunstraum, Leipzig DE 2019, *État Temporaire: Mutagenèse*, 2019, DOC!, Paris, FR, *Unselect/Unlucid*, (s), 2019 KleineHumboldt Galerie, Berlin.

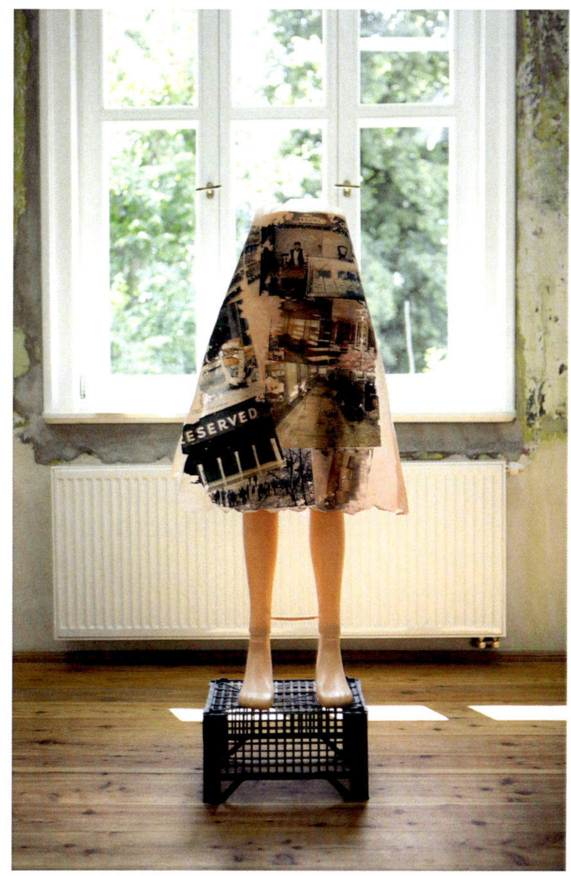

Agnieska Szostek, *Untitled (war doesn't mean the end of fashion. Sanctions on Russia were the inspiration)* 2022, thermoplastic imprint, mannikin.

Acknowledgments

Girls + Eggs is a work of poor curating. I am grateful to the artists in the show for their amazing work, their belief in the project and it's (my) ridiculous humor, and for their grace and flexibility with the idiosyncratic methods of working. The project began without conventional funding and so, together with the co-founders of the orginating venue, CU AT SADKA (Michael Biber and Agnieszka Szosteck), we put a lot of our own resources into making this happen. We spent our own money, expended labor, time, and energy and we gained a deep and lasting friendship. All of this is woven into the fabric of the project itself.

Agnieszka was there from the beginning to the end. She helped me bring *Girls + Eggs* to its final destination in Virginia. I am endlessly delighted by her company, her vivid intelligence, energy, honesty, loyalty, her artistic talent, and her ludicrous humor. Although the inner critic never sleeps, she has the most generous spirit of anyone I know.

Thank you to Beth Hinderliter for inviting me to bring *Girls + Eggs* to JMU. I am grateful for the kind hospitality during the long hours of installation. It was a delight to work with such an empathetic and generous collaborator. Thank you to all the students in the internship program and I am grateful for the support—personal and practical—of the faculty in the art and art history program. A special thank you to MiKyoung Lee, the Director of the School of Art, Design, and Art History.

This catalog has been expanded and enriched by the essays of Jane Marcus-Delgado, Alyson Bardsley, and Beth Hinderliter. Thank you for these politically urgent and thoughtful texts.

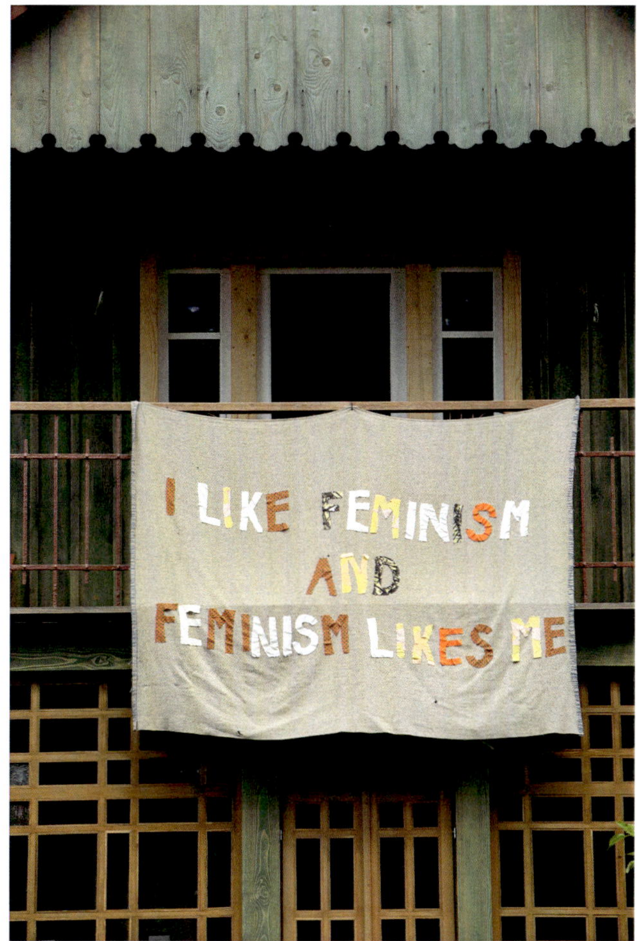

Oskar Korsár and Siona Wilson *I Like Feminism and Feminism Likes me*, 2020, hand stitching on woolen blanket, 65 x 90 inches, seen at CU AT SADKA, 2022.